Raising an Emotionally Intelligent Child

Revolutionary Holistic Strategies to Nurture Your Child's Developing Mind by Cultivating Resilience, Curiosity, Love, and Emotional Wholeness

Serene McLaren

contained within this document, including, but not limited to, errors, omissions, or inaccuracies.

Table of Contents

About the Author

The author of this book, Serene McLaren, is a married woman and a mother of three children. As soon as she became a mother, she inculcated little habits in her life that could be fruitful for raising emotionally intelligent children. She applied those habits and contributed toward making a happy, blended family. She researched children's behavior and how they express themselves in different situations. According to Serene, family is of the utmost importance and the arrival of children makes it more special. Therefore, it is important to understand them and their behaviors to maintain that balance and happiness. She dedicated a lot of time grasping the knowledge on the subject and gained professional expertise. Now a life coach, Serene has helped several parents learn about emotional intelligence and how it works among children. However, she wanted a way that parents from any part of the world could access this information on how to raise an emotionally intelligent child. She worked hard to understand all these emotions and now she is sharing all her knowledge with the readers through this book. With the help of this book, she aims to bridge the gap between parents and children who find it hard to express themselves in front of each other. She wants parents to connect with their children just like she did with hers.

Introduction

Raising a child in this day and age is nothing short of challenging. As a parent, you want nothing more than your child's happiness and well-being; most likely, you find yourself picking up book after book doing as much research as you can to ensure just that. Just take a moment, take a deep breath, and relax. You need not look further for a guide on how to raise your child to ensure that they grow to be healthy and happy individuals. This is it! *Raising an Emotionally Intelligent Child* was written with the single aim to allow you, the parent, to expose your child to all the necessary elements that will allow them to grow to be emotionally intelligent and thus experience all the positive outcomes that accompany it. This book also allows you to develop your emotional intelligence, which will positively impact the family structure and the sense of well-being of the entire household.

This book contains scientifically relevant information in an understandable format to lay the foundation for your understanding of emotional intelligence and the importance thereof. In addition, you will find some fun exercises and assessments to help improve your emotional intelligence and that of your child.

With social media and the increased flow of information that has come with the globalization of our society, you are no longer the only influence in your child's life. There are millions of people on the other side of the world that your child is exposed to while watching YouTube videos, television, and the likes, all of whom can influence the decisions your child may make in the present or future. Most parents report that they experience the greatest amount of stress when thinking about the decisions that their child will be faced with in life. Certain thoughts can be common stressors among all parents, such as, "Will he say NO to drugs?" "Will she practice safe sex?" "Will she make decisions that make her happy?" "Will he be responsible?" Of course, these thoughts are specific to the phase in which your child currently is. Common thoughts among parents of toddlers include, "Will she share her crayons at school today?" "Will she remember to say please and thank you?" "Will he remember to wash his hands after he goes to the bathroom?" "Will he say that bad word again?" "I hope she doesn't take anything that doesn't belong to her again," and the likes. At the same time, parents of children in their 20s might find themselves concerned about their child's choice of university, boyfriend, girlfriend, or friends. The truth is, as parents, you never want your child to make the same mistakes that you do. You impose your beliefs and opinions onto them and hope for the best results. You have been young and foolish, and you'd hate for your child to have the same regrets as you; but what if . . . now, stay with me here . . . there is a better way to ensure that they make the best decisions for themselves?

That's where emotional intelligence comes in!

Simply put, emotional intelligence is the ability to identify, understand, and interpret both your emotions as well as emotions of those that you interact with, so that you may carry out an action best suited to your understanding (Cherry, 2020). Since this comes with monitoring your thoughts as well as your feelings and moods, emotional intelligence is associated with self-awareness and mindfulness, both of which positively impact the decision-making process. Emotionally intelligent individuals are aware of the impact that their actions and decisions will have on themselves and those around them and have shown to make decisions that are in keeping with their chosen belief systems or value systems, even under the influence of peer pressure.

High levels of emotional intelligence are associated with a higher intelligence quotient (IQ) as well as more profound and more honest relationships and improved mental health among individuals (Morin, 2019a).

Before going any further in this book, a few terms need to be defined to help in your understanding. Often the words "emotions," "feelings," and "mood" are used interchangeably when they are, in fact, defined in different ways. According to Joshua Freedman, a co-founder and CEO of the "Six Seconds Emotional Intelligence Network," the difference in these terms is a matter of time. Emotions are a rapid response to a situation; then, feelings develop as time goes by, and eventually, the combination of feelings results in a mood (Freedman, 2017).

Many studies done over the years have shown that lack of emotional control or awareness can lead to irrational behavior and decision making, which can therefore impair an individual's functionality. William James, a well-known American philosopher and psychologist, proposed that emotion is associated with unconscious brain activity that results in a physiological change and action, while feelings require more conscious mental work and are perceptions of emotions (James, 1884). Emotions motivate a person to respond to a stimulus, and feelings are what arise when you take time to think about your emotion; they are subjective expressions of emotion. While this may sound a little convoluted, stay with me. Let's imagine you are hiking in a beautiful forest in the middle of the day. You hear a loud noise that sounds like the cracking of a huge branch and turn around to find a mountain wolf standing in front of you and just staring. Now, since emotion is unconscious and results in physiological change and action, we can rightfully assume that the emotion you would be feeling is fear. Some of the physiological changes that will be caused by the presence of the wolf would be an increased heart rate and blood pressure, sweating or shaking, and an increased breathing rate. An action that could be motivated by your emotion would be to slowly back away. Now, imagine the world has no interest in you and simply turns around and runs away; you have time to consciously think about your experience. The emotion of fear will bring about feelings of helplessness, anxiousness, as well as the feeling of being terrified, scared, and shocked.

The discrete emotion theory claims that there is a small number of core emotions. This concept was studied by many others, and although insufficient to capture all aspects of emotion among humans, there is an understanding that these emotions are displayed using the same facial expressions among individuals of different social, cultural, and ethical groups (Zhang et al., 2014). These emotions include interest, enjoyment, surprise, distress, fear, anger, shame, and disgust (Lindebaum & Jordan, 2012).

Feelings, on the other hand, are vast and varied. Some feelings include:

- Amazed
- Anguish
- Appreciative
- Awe
- Bliss
- Calm
- Centered
- Compassions
- Concerned
- Content
- Depressed
- Empathy
- Enchanted
- Exhausted
- Free

- Happy
- Hopeless
- Humble
- Impotent
- Incapable
- Invigorated
- Involved
- Lively
- Lonely
- Lucky
- Melancholy
- Moved
- Overwhelmed
- Passionate
- Patient

- Peaceful
- Refreshed
- Regretful
- Rejuvenated
- Reluctant
- Remorseful
- Safe
- Satisfied
- Shocked
- Thankful
- Thrilled
- Trapped
- Unhappy
- Upset
- Warm
- Worried

Moods are more generalized and are influenced by your emotions and feelings as well as other factors such as the environment, your physiology, and your mental state. They also may last a longer period of time than emotions or feelings (Freedman, 2017).

Now do you understand why emotions are so important in living a healthy and happy life? Your emotions ultimately play a vital role in your actions.

Another important thing to remember when teaching your child emotional awareness and mindfulness is the power of negative experiences. Although as parents you would love for your child to have only positive experiences and positive emotions, this is unrealistic and can progress into something called "toxic positivity." It's important to understand that negative or unwanted experiences are necessary for growth and development, which can sometimes play a more positive role than a positive experience. Ultimately, what you learn from each experience is more important than the experience itself.

Toxic positivity is the belief that one should maintain a positive outlook regardless of the situation. Guarding yourself and your child against toxic positivity, especially with the youth's current dogma of "good vibes only," is important to prevent living a life of facades and lies. Although it may seem like a stretch, focusing on being positive through difficult situations can quickly lead to ignoring negative emotions and denial. All emotions have their time and place but more about that later.

One last thing before we really get into it. This book is an investment in your child's future to ensure that they are able to make well-informed decisions that will positively influence their well-being and happiness. If you have picked up this book and are reading it right now, I just want you to know, parent to parent, that you are doing a great job! Although as parents we don't really look for recognition or accolades, sometimes it's nice to hear that we're not completely failing, and you are not! In fact, you are succeeding by wanting to improve your parenting techniques and knowledge. Like I said earlier, parenting is not easy, but I daresay it's worth it.

With that said, let's get into *Raising an Emotionally Intelligent Child*!

Chapter 1:

The Anatomy of the Human Brain

Before looking into brain development and the importance of certain activities and exercises, it is important to have a general understanding of the human brain and its function.

Parts of the Human Brain

The brain is the most complex organ in the human body, with each small part being responsible for a multitude of different functions. The structure of the brain as well as its functions have been studied for centuries and continues to be studied to this day. The brain is the control center of our being and the source of all qualities that define humanity. Like all muscles, the brain must be exercised to improve its strength and endurance; targeting specific areas to exercise can help with proficiency in specific activities. In the same way, neglecting certain areas of the brain can lead to weakness and poor proficiency in other areas of life, much like how a paraplegic unable to use his legs will suffer from muscle atrophy. Let's take a quick look at the anatomy of the human brain to get a greater understanding of which areas are responsible for what activities.

Although there are many different parts of the brain, it is universally accepted that the brain can be divided into three main parts or functional units: the forebrain, midbrain, and hindbrain. The hindbrain, situated toward the back of the body as its name suggests, includes the upper part of the spinal cord, the brain stem, and the cerebellum. The cerebellum, Latin for "little brain," is a clump of brain tissue located near the brain stem and is responsible for coordinating voluntary movement and motor skills such as balance and posture. Activities such as catching a ball or playing an instrument activates the cerebellum and makes it stronger. The hindbrain as a whole is known to control vital bodily functions such as heart rate, sleep-wake cycles, and respiration rate (National Institute of Neurological Disorders and Stroke, 2020).

The midbrain is the topmost portion of the brain stem and is situated between the forebrain and hindbrain. This area of the brain serves important functions in motor movement, especially that of the eyes, and in auditory and visual processing (Encyclopedia Britannica, 2016).

The forebrain is the largest and most highly developed part of the human brain and consists primarily of the cerebrum and the "inner brain," the structures directly beneath the cerebrum. It is the bulk of the brain and the source of intellectual activities. It controls initiation of movement, touch, hearing, judgment, reasoning, problem solving, emotions, and learning (John Hopkins Medicine, 2019). It also holds memories, allows you to imagine and think, and controls other physiological factors such as temperature (National Institute of Neurological Disorders and Stroke, 2020).

The Cerebrum

Being the bulk of the brain, the cerebrum is usually what people see when looking at a diagram or picture of a brain. It is split straight down the middle to form the left and right hemispheres, and although similar in image, both hemispheres are different in function. Some brain functions reside more on one side of the brain than the other. The left brain is usually associated with language, analytical thinking, logic, and general order while the right brain is associated with imagination, intuition, rhythm, creativity, and artistic ability. This is why sometimes individuals are classed as dominant in either the left or right brain. Having said this, evidence of the theory that one side of your brain may be dominant over the other is almost nonexistent. In fact, it has been proven that it is almost impossible for one side of your brain to function independent of the other side. Nevertheless, one side of your brain can be stronger than the other side, depending on what activities you engage in when exercising your brain (Shmerling, 2017).

When signals are sent to the brain via chemical transmitters released by neurons (nerve cells), the information crosses hemispheres to reach the opposite one to the side of the body that is transmitting the signal. This means that the right hemisphere controls the left side of the body, and vice versa.

The cerebral hemispheres can be further divided into various sections called lobes, which also have specialized function. These are the frontal, parietal, occipital, and temporal lobes.

The Frontal Lobes

The frontal lobe of the cerebrum is located directly behind the forehead and are large lobes with many functions. These lobes are considered our emotional control center and are believed to play a role in our personalities as well as manage executive functions such as problem solving, decision making, and behavioral control. The back portion of the left frontal lobe is called the Broca's area and is known as the language center of the brain. Paul Broca, the French neurosurgeon, is known to have exclaimed "we speak with the left hemisphere" right when he discovered the area and its functions. In addition, the rearmost portion of each frontal lobe is a motor area which helps control voluntary movement (The Brain from Top to Bottom, 2019).

Here are some interesting facts about the frontal lobes (Saladi-Schulman, 2020):

- They are the largest lobes of your brain. They are situated at the center of your brain and make up around one third of your brain.

- The frontal lobes are the largest of your brain's lobes. They're in the foreground of your mind. They are thought to make up around a third of your brain.

- Primates, including humans, have a substantially larger frontal lobe than other species. You may claim that the frontal lobe is the most crucial part of our brain for different "human" abilities like reasoning and communication.

- The frontal lobes are strongly connected to other parts of the brain via neural connections, emphasizing their significance in a wide range of functions. If any damage occurs to the frontal lobes, it may have a "ripple effect" on other areas of the brain.

The Parietal Lobes

The lobes right behind the frontal lobes are called the parietal lobes, and the foremost part of these lobes are the primary sensory areas of the brain. These areas receive and process information about taste, touch, temperature, and movement. They tell us where our body is in relation to objects around us and allow us to move without bumping into things. In addition, these areas of the brain are involved in processing information for mathematical and spelling skills as well as hand-eye coordination and fine motor skills such as those required to tie a shoelace (Headway, 2018). Just like the brain, the central furrow, or medial longitudinal fissure, divides the parietal lobe into two hemispheres. The parietal lobe receives information from various parts of the body. For example, your skin and its nerves play an important role in identifying sensory information and transferring it to the parietal lobe.

Navigation and bodily control, as well as recognizing spatial orientation and direction, are all processes that the parietal lobe is involved in. What part of the parietal lobe is more responsive is often determined by a person's dominant hand. Right-handed people are likely to have a more robust parietal lobe in the left hemisphere. The left lobe is more active in handling letters, numbers, and symbols. In individuals who have a dominant left hand, the right hemisphere may be more functional. The right hemisphere is linked to image analysis and spatial connections. These characteristics, however, do not apply to the other side of the lobe. Everyone uses both the left and right hemisphere of the parietal lobe as well as the brain.

The Occipital Lobes

These are the two hindmost lobes of the cerebrum and play a role in vision and visual perception. They process images from the eyes and refer to memory in order to make sense of this information (John Hopkins Medicine, 2019). Each one of the four parts of the occipital lobe is accountable for a specific visual function. The occipital lobe gets its name because it is located below the occipital bone of your skull. This lobe is the smallest in size. There are two occipital lobes in the brain, one in each hemisphere. These lobes are divided and separated by the central cerebral fissure. The occipital lobes are found in the rear part of your upper brain. They are located above the cerebellum, behind the parietal and temporal lobes and are separated from the cerebellum by a membrane known as the tentorium cerebelli.

The occipital lobe is associated with several aspects of vision, like:

- Distance

- Color identification

- Object recognition

- Depth perception

- Movement

- Memory data

- Face recognition

Humans have binocular perception because both occipital lobes of the hemispheres get visual input from both retinas. Since this merges two images into one in the brain, it helps in providing more depth and spatial awareness of your surroundings (Johnson, 2020). However, the visual world is extremely complicated. As a result, decoding this information is a complex job.

The Temporal Lobes

These are the lobes that lie underneath the parietal and frontal lobes and in front of the occipital lobe. They are located on the side of your brain, just above your ears. The posterior portion of the left temporal lobe is involved in understanding language and is referred to as Wernicke's area. It is associated with the processing of words that are heard and spoken and connects to the Broca's area with a large bundle of nerve fibers (Encyclopedia Britannica, 2019). These lobes are important to process and understand sounds such as music as well as manage emotions, recognize faces, and with short-term memory (The Urban Child Institute, 2009).

There are three key structures of the temporal lobe:

- Broca's area

- Wernicke's area

- limbic system

These structures also cross other lobes. For instance, Broca's area is also a part of the frontal lobe, whereas Wernicke's area is a part of the parietal lobe. The main auditory complex is located in the temporal lobe. This is the first region in the brain that processes messages from the ears in the form of sounds. The temporal lobe interprets the meaning of varied sounds, frequencies, and pitches received from the ears. In humans, the temporal nerve is associated with selective hearing. Selective hearing lets a person focus on the relevant sounds in their environment by filtering out the unwanted frequencies. The temporal lobe also has a visual component. It helps establish object detection, including complex items like faces. Finally, the temporal lobe is involved in language comprehension and interpretation. This makes language understandable and distinguishable.

The Cerebral Cortex

The cerebral cortex refers to the thin layer of the brain that covers the cerebrum. The cortex is referred to as gray matter because the nerves in this area of the brain do not have the insulation that allows the other areas of the brain to appear white; the functions of this layer include thought, memory, sensory perception, and voluntary action. This layer contains a large number of folds which gives the brain it's well-known appearance and serves to increase the surface area so that more information can be processed in a shorter period of time (National Institute of Neurological Disorders and Stroke, 2020). The surface of the cerebral cortex is widely folded, generating ridges known as gyri and valleys known as sulci. The folding permits the surface area to be substantially increased, allowing more neurons to be accommodated. The cerebral cortex is divided into two hemispheres by a huge sulcus referred to as the medial longitudinal fissure.

The cerebral cortex is commonly divided into three types of sections for ease of understanding: motor, sensory, and association areas. While motor and sensory areas are certainly important for good cognition and behavior, association areas are also extremely significant. Association areas are found across the cortex and play a role in the integration of data from various parts of the brain. This integration can assist complicated cognitive functions like language, artistic expression, and decision making (National Institute of Neurological Disorders and Stroke, 2020).

Inner Structures of the Brain

There are many parts of the brain that exist deep under its surface which play important roles in our functionality as human beings.

The hypothalamus is a pea-shaped unit that controls our sleep-wake cycles, the release of certain hormones in your body, and is an important emotion center. The thalamus lies above the hypothalamus and is involved in the processing of information between the spinal cord and cerebrum. The hippocampus is a tiny nub that is the memory center of our brains.

The Neuron

Neurons are nerve cells that transmit data to other neuron cells, gland cells, and muscle cells. Most neurons contain an axon, cell body, and dendrites. The axon is the output structure of neurons; whenever a neuron wishes to communicate with another neuron, it transmits an electrical message throughout the axon. The nucleus, which houses the neuron's DNA, and where proteins are created to be carried throughout the axon and dendrites, are all located in the soma. The mature brain consists of over 100 billion neurons that process the information to and from the brain. Neurons don't regenerate or reproduce like other cells. Therefore, once they get damaged, they can't be replaced into new ones. Neurons make connections with one another, and the point of this connection is referred to as a synapse. These cells are the basic functional units of the brain and are electrically excitable, meaning that they are easily activated by small changes in the surrounding ionic environment. The central nervous system consists of the brain, and the spinal cord contains a significantly large number of neurons as well that receive sensory information and relay motor information.

The production of new nerve cells is known as neurogenesis. While the process itself is not clearly understandable yet, it may be present in some parts of the brain after birth. While a lot of research has been done in the last decade to better understand the neurons, there is still a lot to discover. For example, until a recent study, researchers thought that the creation of neurons in adults occurred in a region of the brain called the hippocampus. However, the recent study put the theory of hippocampus neurogenesis into question. Researchers analyzed the hippocampus samples from 37 donors and concluded that adults produce relatively less hippocampal neurons than usual (Vandergriendt, 2018). Though the results have not been confirmed yet, they come with a critical drawback. Many scientists were hopeful that neurogenesis could help treat diseases like Parkinson's and Alzheimer's, which are the main cause of neuron damage.

Connections and Communication

Information is received, sent out, and processed via cells called neurons, which release chemical signals called neurotransmitters in order to relay messages to and from the different parts of the body and the brain. These chemical signals are released by stimulation of these nerve cells via electrical impulses. Groups of these neurons found within the body in areas except for the brain, such as the legs and arms, are referred to as nerves. Stepping on a thorn, for example, sends nerve impulses from your foot to your spinal cord that causes you to pull your leg up in pain. Looking at a delicious piece of pizza allows your brain to process what you are seeing, activate the part of your brain that will make the decision to eat the pizza, and then send a signal to the part of your brain that is responsible for voluntary movement and coordination so that you can reach for the pizza and lift it to your mouth.

A neural pathway is a group of neurons that communicate at their synapses to send information from one part of the brain to another and are created in the brain based on our habits and behaviors. As a person engages in a new activity more often and trains their brain to become more familiar with the action of catching a ball or playing the piano, new neural pathways are created which get stronger with repetition. Soon, these activities will come easier to the individual and require less energy and focus.

Now that you have a basic understanding of the parts of the brain, let's look at how the brain of a child develops from the fetal phase all the way into infancy.

Chapter 2:

An Overview of Brain

Development

Kids are born ready to study and have a long list of talents to master. They look up to their parents, relatives, and other guardians as their first educators in order to gain the skills they need to become self-sufficient and live healthy and prosperous lives. The way a child's brain develops is heavily influenced by his or her interactions with society and the world. Therefore, the importance of mind-nurturing care is crucial for brain development.

Human brain development is known to begin during the third gestational week and continue throughout early childhood. The general structure of the brain is developed with time, beginning before birth and ending far into adulthood. A child's brain develops at a faster rate from birth to age five than at any other period in life. A child's ability to understand and achieve in school and at home is influenced by brain development. The nature of a child's early experiences, whether favorable or unfavorable, has an impact on how their brain grows. Childhood experiences influence the quality of that structure by laying a solid or unstable basis for all learning skills, health, and behavior. Every second, around one million new brain connections are established in the first few years (Harvard University, 2019). After this time of rapid growth, connections are pruned to make brain circuits more functional. The first sensory pathways to emerge are those for fundamental vision and hearing, followed by early verbal skills and advanced cognitive abilities. Later, more sophisticated brain circuits are built upon previous, simpler circuits, and connections multiply and prune in a predefined sequence.

There is some argument about whether brain development ever actually stops or continues throughout the duration of our lives. By definition, the word "develop" means to grow and become more mature, advanced, or elaborate, so one might argue that since we become more mature and advanced through our life experiences and the lessons we learn, our brain is in fact developing right until the moment that we take our very last breath. Those who believe that our brains cease to develop further at a certain age argue that exercising certain areas of the brain, such as those that are involved in memory or intellectual ability, is not necessarily further developing the brain but rather utilizing the developed parts that are already present. Whichever you believe, we can all agree that the brain is an organ that leaves us in awe of our potential as the human race.

A common misconception that is fueled by the growing world of science fiction is that we use a mere 10% of our brains. This is, in fact, a myth that has been extorted to further the narrative of marketing experts and the world of Hollywood. Researchers have shown that most of our brain is active almost all of the time, even when performing little tasks that require small amounts of voluntary coordination and attention (Hughes et al., 2013).

At birth, the size of a baby's brain is about a quarter of the size that it will grow to be. Within the first year, the brain will just about double in size, and by age three, it would have grown to about 80% of its full size. Although structural changes continue throughout childhood, it has been proven that by age six, a child's brain is about 90% of its adult size and volume (Lenroot & Giedd, 2006).

Immediately after birth, and in the six months following, the level of connectivity throughout the brain exceeds that of adults. This is to allow for the child to learn and grow by observation and experience and explains why plasticity and capacity for adaptation is the hallmark of early brain development (Stiles & Jernigan, 2010).

Brain Development in the Womb

Around the end of the second week of pregnancy, the embryo in a woman's womb is a small oval-shaped structure that consists only of two layers. Around the third week, the embryo undergoes a process called gastrulation during which the structure is transformed into a three-layered one—when the cells of the upper layer, the epiblast cells, will differentiate into the three primary stem cell lines and develop into all the structures in the developing embryo. The neural stem cells are the cells that will eventually produce the cells that make up the brain and spinal cord (Stiles & Jernigan, 2010).

Then, during the third week of pregnancy, the neural tube forms from neural stem cells, and a single layer of cells line the center of the tube. At this stage, the tube looks somewhat like a straw—it will grow and develop into a fully functional brain in due time. The upper part of the tube will grow into the brain while the lower part will grow into the hindbrain and spinal cord. By the end of the embryonic period of growth, at about week eight of pregnancy, major differentiation of the neural tube has occurred and different segments of the embryonic brain are visible (Stiles & Jernigan, 2010).

The fetal period of development usually refers to the period between week nine and the end of pregnancy or gestation. During this period, the brain undergoes major structural and functional changes. At the beginning, the brain began as a smooth structure that began to differentiate into different functional units. Now, the formation of folds begins to occur to give the brain its well-known appearance. These folds are called gyri and sulci; gyri are the bumps and sulci are the indentations or grooves. Primary sulci are formed first and are followed by secondary branches, tertiary branches, as well as the deep groove that separates the two hemispheres called the primary fissure.

Neuron production begins around day 42 of pregnancy and forms neural network pathways. The billions of neurons that an adult possesses within their brain are produced around the middle of the gestational period. The brain becomes larger as it develops, and as the different layers of the cortex grow, they contain different types of neurons. It's important to note that neurogenesis, the actual process by which neurons are formed in the brain, occurs only to a limited degree after birth.

Around week eight, the corpus callosum, a bundle of neural fibers that connect the left and right hemispheres of the brain, begins to differentiate. This structure is completely formed by about week 20. In the second half of gestation, astrocytes, a type of support cells for the neurons, develop. These cells play a major role in transmission and processing of information and are in close contact with blood vessels for supply of nutrients to the brain. Oligodendrocytes, structural support cells for neurons, reach peak formation around week 15, and the formation of synapses begins before week 27.

When a baby is born, although the brain is completely formed and fully functional, neurons are unable to communicate efficiently via synapses. The cerebral cortex produces most of its synaptic connections after birth. At around age three, the brain has almost twice as many synapses and neural pathways as it will have in adulthood, as these connections are gradually lost during growth.

Genes control the movement of newly formed neurons to ensure that they settle where they belong. They allow the brain to receive information about the environment and stimulate neural activity. The amount of information received increases the number of synapses between neurons and activates certain areas of the brain repetitively. For example, if a newborn baby hears the sound of a bird outside the window, the auditory areas of the brain will activate. If the baby hears the sound of her mother's voice, the auditory and speech areas of the brain will be activated, and more synapses will develop. Repeated activation of areas of the brain strengthens the synapses and thus development of those areas.

During the first year of life, the cerebellum triples in size which is known to be due to the repeated activation of this area during the development of motor skills. The visual areas of the cortex also grow to improve the child's ability to see and absorb more of his/her environment.

The growth in the hippocampus that occurs within the first three months of life improves the powers of recognition of the child as well as the limbic system and memory. Within the first year, language circuits in the frontal and temporal lobes also become consolidated after constant activation by listening to the language of those around. Studies have shown that a baby in an English-speaking home is able to distinguish between the sounds of a foreign language during the first year of life—a skill which is lost as the years go on (Kuhl, 2000).

During the second year of life, there are more dramatic and significant changes in the language areas of the brain. During this time, there is also an increase in myelination of the neurons in the brain. This is basically the growth of a layer of insulation over the neurons in the brain that act to increase the speed of nerve impulses as well. This increase in myelination results in the improvement in cognitive abilities and more complex tasks. It is at this stage that self-awareness begins to develop, so emotional intelligence can also be developed.

During the third year of life, the neural connections throughout the brain strengthen, and memory as well as cognitive abilities improve.

While the number of connections between cells in the brain is significantly more before age of three as compared to an adult, it requires too much energy to maintain these connections, so as a child grows, their brain optimizes the necessary connections while allowing some to simply fall away (Wessel, 2019).

Emotional Factors Influencing Brain Development

Emotion has a great influence on the cognitive process in people, including learning, perception, attention, reasoning, memory, and problem solving. Emotion has a particularly significant impact on attention, influencing attention selectivity, as well as inspiring behavior and action. Since naturally limited attentional abilities are better centered on necessary information, this attentional and executive control is directly related to learning procedures. Emotion also helps in the efficient storing and retrieving information.

As experiences are the basis for brain development, one question arises: How does one experience the life they are leading? From a neuroscience standpoint, it would predominantly include the five senses: smell, taste, touch and vibration, hearing, and vision. We are born into a sensory environment in which we are hugged, caressed, stroked, kissed, hummed to, talked to, massaged, fed, and loved—in other words, nurtured. We nurture and nourish our brain through these activities so that it develops and keeps the connections we would need to move forward.

The "Serve and Return" Relationship

According to scientists, the most important factor that affects a child's brain development is the "serve and return" relationship between parents and children and other caregivers in the family or society (Harvard University, 2019). A child's holistic development requires meaningful relationships with responsive, trusted adults. These relations start at home, with family and relatives, but they extend to teachers, childcare providers, and other people involved with the child. Since parents spend the most time with their child, they are responsible for generating positive experiences that will prepare their child to adapt and adjust in the outer world. Other relatives like siblings, aunts, uncles, family friends, and caregivers can all act as a shield and provide positive reinforcement as the child learns new skills to thrive and succeed.

Children find different ways to communicate with their parents or other caregivers from the moment they are born. For example, when a baby cries or fusses, consistent responses from their caregivers bring them comfort, and they expect similar responses in the future. Each one of these little signals gives a chance to the caregiver to be responsive to the needs of the child. Babbling, facial expressions, and gestures are normal ways for young children to seek engagement, and adults respond with the same vocalizing and gesturing.

As the child grows to experience similar things, their expectations strengthen, creating perceptions of the emotional and social world in which they live. These perceptions have an impact on how babies perceive their surroundings, interact with others, and learn. When those experiences are mostly pleasant, children interpret other people's actions and signals positively and are driven to learn more about the world. Parents or caregivers who pay attention to their children, respond to them, and connect with them are actually shaping their brains. That's why it's crucial to chat, play, sing, and enjoy with children from the moment they are born, to allow them to experience their material world as well as provide them with secure, stable, and supportive situations.

The Age Factor

With aging, the brain's ability to change reduces. Early in life, the brain is most adaptable, or "plastic," to a variety of areas and events, but as it matures and becomes more specialized to perform more complicated functions, it becomes less susceptible to reorganizing and adjusting to different or unexpected difficulties. By the first year, the areas of the brain that distinguish sound are being tailored to the language the newborn has been introduced to, while the brain is already losing the ability to recognize distinct sounds available in other languages. Although the opportunities for learning languages and other abilities stay open, it becomes more difficult to change these brain circuits with time. Due to early plasticity, influencing a baby's developing brain structure is easier and more successful than rewiring parts of its circuitry in adulthood.

The Toxic Stress Damage

Toxic stress harms the architecture of the developing brain, which can result in learning, behavior, and physical and mental health issues later in life. According to scientists, chronic, unremitting stress in early life, caused by dire conditions, frequent abuse, or extreme maternal depression, is now known to be harmful to the brain development, While positive stress (mild, short-term physiological reactions to unpleasant experiences) is an essential and critical part of healthy growth, toxic stress is the natural, unrelieved stimulation of the body's stress management system. In the absence of cushioning adult support, toxic stress is generated into the body through mechanisms that change the circuitry of the developing brain (McEwen, 2011).

According to neuroscience, the absence of meaningful interactions in childhood has been linked to a lower brain volume and a lack of neural connections in the brain. Neuroscientists have also discovered that the behavioral patterns we encounter as children become encoded in our brains and influence how we interact with people throughout our lives. Poor brain development and traumatic childhood events can have long-term implications. They might include a lack of compassion, rigid attitudes and behaviors, interpersonal difficulties, and the emergence of a variety of personality disorders (National Research Council (US) and Institute of Medicine (US) Committee on Integrating the Science of Early Childhood Development, 2000).

There are presently four personality disorders that are known to cause people to act violently or selfishly. These are psychopathy, antisocial personality disorder, narcissistic personality disorder, and paranoid personality disorder. While the exact cause of these diseases is unknown, it is extremely likely that emotionally or physically abusive relationships during childhood and adolescence play a role in their development. Of course, not every child who has been neglected or abused will grow up to have a serious personality problem. That is ensured by the human spirit's resiliency. However, a small percentage of people do, and it is this minority that is to blame for the majority of the excessive greed and violence.

Although the first five years of a child's life is vital in brain development, new neural pathways are made regularly as a child is exposed to new activities that require different areas of their brain. It's important to expose your child to a variety of different activities so that they can continue to develop the various areas of their brains. More importantly, the emotional and social skills that a child develops during their foundation years will determine their successes in later life.

Chapter 3:

Where to Start

Parenting is tough, but it was never supposed to be easy! Most times, parents get tired of the not-so-good habits of their children and are not able to make any sense of that behavior. Of course, as a parent, you want the best for your child. You want them to grow up into someone with a strong personality, realizing their true potential, be emotionally intelligent, and be kind toward other people. You want them to have good grades, meaningful relationships, and be disciplined rather than being annoying and troublesome. Yet, think about it for a second from their perspective. Are they throwing all those tantrums intentionally? What would you have done if you were in their place? What do you do when they get all cranky? You probably bribe them with something they like if they behave well. This is where we, as parents, are mistaken. We try to control their tantrums using submission instead of teaching them how to change their actions and behavior for the better.

It takes more than intelligence to be a good parent. It focuses on a part of the personality that has been overlooked in much of the parenting advice given out in the last three decades. Emotions play a role in good parenting. Science has learned a lot about the part emotions play in our lives in the last 10 years or so (John Mordechai Gottman et al., 2015). Researchers have discovered that your emotional intelligence and ability to manage emotions will influence your success and happiness in many aspects of life, including family relations. For parents, this attribute of "emotional intelligence" means being conscious of your child's emotions and being able to sympathize, calm, and guide them. (Gottman et al., 2015)

According to Daniel Goleman, psychologist and author of Emotional Intelligence,

Family life is our first school for emotional learning. In this intimate cauldron we learn how to feel about ourselves and how others will react to our feelings; how to think about these feelings and what choices we have in reacting; how to read and express hopes and fears. This emotional schooling operates not just through the things parents say and do directly to children, but also in the models they offer for handling their own feelings and those that pass between husband and wife. Some parents are gifted emotional teachers, others atrocious. (Gottman et al., 2015)

Raising your child emotionally is about encouraging and nurturing your child in a peaceful manner that gives them guidance and recognition. It is about setting boundaries, rewarding them for their good behavior, and making them realize the bad ones using mindful techniques rather than punishment.

Emotional Training

What happens when you give your children emotional training? Emotional training entails being a mentor or teacher to your child, being sensitive toward their feelings and showing care, supporting and motivating them to become independent, being affectionate, helping them differentiate between negative and positive emotions, and encouraging healthy communication. Children whose parents perform emotion training on a regular basis could have better health and academic success than those who do not provide such guidance. These children get on well with their friends, have fewer behavioral issues, and are less likely to engage in violent activity. In general, emotion-coached children have fewer negative emotions and happier feelings. In a nutshell, they're more emotionally balanced.

Emotional training doesn't mean that discipline is no longer necessary, but when you are emotionally closer to your child, you get more involved in their lives and thus have a stronger influence over them.

You can still be tough when the situation demands it. Since you have an emotional bond with your children, even if you are a little tough on them, they will mark your words and realize their mistakes. This way, emotional training can help you motivate and guide your kids in the right direction. Emotional training needs the right amount of patience and commitment, but the task is just like that of a coach. If you want your kid to be good at sports, you practice the game with them, not avoid it. In the same way, if you want your kid to manage his feelings, deal with negative emotions, and maintain healthy relationships, you guide them instead of scolding or pushing them away. While relatives, educators, and other caretakers can be emotion coaches in a child's development, as a parent, you are in the best position to do so. Besides, you are the one who decides what boundaries your child should follow, and you are the one who will be there for them when things go rough. Whether it's potty training, infant colic, sibling issues, or missed homecoming dates, your child turns to you for guidance.

Emotional training strengthens the bond between you and your child and shapes the personality of your child, behaviors, making them clearer about their interests and choices.

The kind of connection you have with your child will determine the type of communication and responses they will have. It will also determine their social, emotional, and mental health. Children who grow up in an environment full of loving parents and relatives are more likely to bond with other people. They tend to put more effort in their relationships and fulfill them as opposed to a child growing up in a negative environment. A child who can talk about his feelings openly to his parents without any hesitation is better in dealing with problems and handling his emotions better.

There are a lot of benefits of having a child-parent relationship:

- It improves the mental, linguistic, and cognitive growth of the child.

- It improves his social and academic skills.

- It allows the child to become more optimistic and confident.

- The child feels more motivated and driven to face whatever challenges come his way.

- It helps develop strong problem-solving skills and also gives them the ability to ask someone for help.

Steps to Get Started on the Right Foot

As a parent, you must have a lot of questions about where to start from when it comes to raising an emotionally intelligent child. To give you a road map, here are some tips:

Start Early

They say that the moment a woman becomes pregnant, she starts to develop a loving bond with her unborn child. Fathers, on the other hand, feel like fathers later in the process, when they carry their newborn in their arms for the first time. According to research, fathers who have a connection with their children during their early age are more likely to keep a stronger bond when their children grow older. (Sarkadi et al., 2007). Hence, rule number one to strengthen your bond with your child is to be involved with them from the start.

Be Responsive

Children are like explorers. They encounter thousands of things everyday which surprise them, overwhelm, or excite them in a way. Then starts the never-ending trail of whats and whys. In this case, instead of avoiding their questions or asking them to stop, your job is to be responsive to their curious and fun questions. Of course, there are some days where you are not feeling your best and facing some issues in your life, but as a parent, saying "no" to a child is probably one of the biggest mistakes you can make. You saying no gives them a sense of disinterest and makes them feel that you don't care. They feel unheard and ignored, so it's crucial to be attentive to their needs and curiosities. You need to visualize things from their perspective and feel the sense of excitement they are feeling.

Give Them the Utmost Priority

Your interaction and involvement with your child should be on the top of your list, ALL THE TIME! Children pick up and adapt the behaviors they see or feel around them and form similar connections. A parent who doesn't care much about his child is likely to experience the same behavior from his child when he grows up. Therefore, it's important for you to show them that you care about them and love them. Spend some quality time with them, take care of their health and well-being, and pay attention to their problems—no matter how little they are—and listen to them when they come to you asking for help. Instead of setting up your priorities based on your other commitments and taking only some time out for them, try setting your priorities that revolve around them. Make them your priority!

Talk to Them

Try to be more communicative and open with your child. Talk to them about even the smallest of things and show them that whenever they need to talk, you are there for them. Keep in mind that the mode of your conversation should be friendly, supportive, and full of care. However, if you want to teach them to be disciplined from the start, make sure to lay some exceptions and ground rules. For instance, you can ask to address any elder with respect, be open to listen to their opinions and advice, and act accordingly. You shouldn't be too laid back about their habits, and you should make sure that they respect your decisions.

Show Interest

Show more interest in their conversations instead of just responding with one-word answers. Sometimes, our children come to us with important information or concerns, which we don't care about much, thinking they are too young to be raising such issues. Sometimes, kids have to deal with major concerns all alone, and that affects both their physical and mental health. They may not be able to talk it out, but they do show some signs. Your job is to notice those signs and figure out a solution. For instance, if you notice something different in your child's behavior such as their communication or gestures, talk to them. Find out if anything is troubling and listen to them. When a child is upset, angry, or terrified, he wants his parents the most. Being able to calm an agitated child is what makes us feel more like parents. By addressing our children's feelings, we are assisting them in developing self-soothing abilities that will benefit them for the rest of their lives.

While some parents try to suppress their children's negative feelings in the hopes that they will disappear, they rarely do. Negative feelings fade away as youngsters are able to talk about, label, and understand their emotions. As a result, it makes sense to acknowledge significantly lower levels of emotions soon before they erupt into a full-blown crisis.

Empathize

Empathy is the capability to understand and feel what the other person is going through. When we witness our children crying, we may imagine ourselves in their shoes and experience their pain as compassionate parents. We can feel our children's frustration and anger as we watch them stomp their feet in fury. As a parent, it is essential for you to empathize with your child and allow them to express their feelings without hesitation. If we can explain this level of personal emotional awareness to them, we can give support to our children 's emotions and encourage them to learn to comfort themselves. Don't demoralize them or tell them to get used to it when they are on the brink of crying. Instead, tell them to let it all out, whatever they are feeling. Help them channel their emotions in the right direction and tell them how to deal with their feelings when they are overwhelmed. This can be a great way to start building emotional intelligence in your child. It will teach them how to handle different emotions and how to be more empathetic.

When we begin to understand what our children are going through, they feel more secure. They are aware that we are on their side. They welcome us into their world when we don't criticize them, dismiss their sentiments, or try to divert them from their ambitions. They express their emotions to us. They convey their viewpoints. Their goals become less enigmatic, leading to a deeper understanding.

Show Respect

Respect is another important aspect of raising an emotionally intelligent child. Although they are not adults, they prefer to be treated like one. Think about it for a second: Do they ask for the same snacks or drinks you have? Do they get annoyed when you drink in a fancy wine glass and all they get is a milk bottle? Kids like to feel acknowledged and valued. They want others to listen to and value their opinions. They want respect for their beliefs, ideas, and thoughts, and if you don't offer them that, you become a bad parent in their eyes. Children require practice weighing possibilities and coming up with answers. They must observe what happens when they make decisions depending on their family's principles; they must also observe what happens when they choose to disregard family standards. These lessons might be difficult, but with emotion training, they can be effective ways for parents to provide direction. Parents should ensure that the sooner a child learns to communicate his or her opinions and make sound decisions, the better.

Encourage

Parents who are well-intentioned individuals whittle away at their children's ego by continually correcting their manners, mocking their errors, and pointing out their flaws, unduly interfering with children's attempts to do the most basic activities. They carelessly label their children with names that cling to the child's skin like glue. Thus, it's important to boost their ego when they are giving their best, even if they are not doing any good. The idea is to motivate them to keep trying without giving up. Everyone needs some form of validation at some point, and children are no different. We all feel disheartened when things don't go our way, and we need a support system to get us through those times. For your children, you are that support system. Encouraging your child helps boost their confidence and self-esteem. Show them that their efforts are valued and will never go to waste. Criticism is also essential but only when the child repeats the same mistakes multiple times.

Show Interest

It is important to show involvement and interest in the things your child is doing. For example, if they are in school, get involved in knowing about their friends, academics, and relations with other people. Keep a record of how he is doing in school through his teachers and caregivers.

Share Their Dreams

This method is a wonderful approach to get on your child's frequency and help them empathize with you. It's especially useful when children express wishes that aren't realistically possible. Let's say your child expresses an interest in a new mountain bike, but you're not able to afford it. If you're like most parents, your first reaction may be frustration. You may want to remind him, "I just bought you a new race bike last year. Do you think I'm a millionaire?"

Think about what would happen if you only considered his wish and engaged in his dream for a few minutes. Then you may reply something like, "Yeah, I can see why you want a mountain bike. You enjoy hiking on the trails, right?" You could even go one step further and say, "Wouldn't it be awesome if all your buddies had mountain bikes as well? Consider what it would be like if I could take a group of you camping for a week. We'd pack our tents, fishing equipment, and . . ." From here, you can consider the advantages of camping with and without mountain bikes. You can still insist that you won't pay for the bike personally, but you might consider brainstorming methods for your kid to earn money to help pay for it. What matters is that your kid understands you have acknowledged them and that you believe their wants are reasonable.

The minds of children are naturally designed to seek safety and affection, as well as knowledge and insight. Your child aspires to be loving and selfless. He wants to learn about the environment, what produces lightning, and what goes on inside an animal. He is curious about what is fair and right, as well as what is wrong and evil. He wants to learn about the world's problems and how to prevent them. He is adamant about doing the right thing and growing stronger and more capable. Your child aspires to be the person you respect and adore. With all these forces, as a parent, you can appreciate your child's sentiments and realize that you are not alone.

Chapter 4:

Why Is Emotional Intelligence

Important?

After reading the introduction, you must have gotten an idea about what emotional intelligence is and how it comes into play for your child's development. We shall continue that in this chapter and find out how important emotional intelligence is in raising a child.

The Theory of Emotional Intelligence

Daniel Goleman, author of Emotional Intelligence and Social Intelligence: The New Science of Human Relationships, defines emotional intelligence as, "the capacity for recognizing our own feelings and those of others, for motivating ourselves, and for managing emotions well in ourselves and in our relationships" (Paavola, 2017). The theory of emotional intelligence first came into existence in 1990, and a number of hypotheses evolved under its name. Today, three basic models of EI exist: the ability or talent model (Mayer & Salovey, 1990), the trait EI model (Petrides & Furnham, 2003), and the mixed models (Bar-On, 2006; Boyatzis & Sala, 2004; Brackett, 2009). According to Mayer and Salovey, emotional intelligence is "the ability to understand, express and organize emotions" (Arslan, 2013).

Talent or Ability Model

Mayer and Salovey's talent model can be divided into the following elements (Mayer & Salovey, 1990):

Perception: It is the ability to recognize and understand emotions. It comprises the ability to recognize and understand emotions communicated through the face, speech, and other forms of communication.

Help: It is described as providing emotional support by taking into account the signals and repercussions of emotions.

Understanding: Knowing the connection between feelings and thinking might help you make better judgments. Emotions can be used to support numerous problem-solving approaches. Emotional signs are described in terms of time, context, and connection, interpreting emotions, being conscious of their tendencies with time, and understanding their outcomes.

Managing: This element is the strength of your personality, which gives you the ability to understand and handle your emotions effectively. Emotions are influenced by one's goals, awareness, and self-definition. Even children are taught to count up to 10 when angry. As people get older, they also get the ability to control their feelings and achieve self-reliance. Salovey sums up emotional abilities into five categories:

1. Self-recognition: Self-recognition or self-awareness is the foundation of emotional intelligence. People who are able to interpret their feelings can better manage their lives and make better life decisions.

2. Managing feelings: This skill is being nurtured in a selfless manner. It is the capacity to correctly regulate feelings. While the weak expend their energy constantly battling restlessness, the strong are able to carry on with their lives cheerfully by

composing themselves easily after encountering life's misfortunes.

3. Keeping yourself motivated: This is the ability to redirect one's feelings toward a goal, as well as the ability to act, be self-controlling, and creative. Those who have these skills are much more efficient and successful.

4. Having a sense of empathy: It is the ability to sympathize with others. People with empathetic skills are able to respond better to and are more sensible to the needs of others.

5. Making connections with people: Those with this ability are able to build effective connections with advanced people in every aspect and maintain a good and successful social life.

Mixed and Trait EI Models

Unlike the ability model, mixed models connect mental skills with personal characteristics like positivity, determination, and stress endurance to provide a comprehensive definition of EI. The Boyatzis-Goleman and Bar-On models of emotional-social intelligence are the two most extensively utilized mixed models. EI skills are divided into four categories by the Boyatzis-Goleman model (Livesey, 2017): self-management, self-awareness, social awareness, and relationship management. Similarly, the five main elements of EI in the Bar-On (2006) model are adaptability, stress management, intrapersonal skills, interpersonal skills. The creators of the trait EI define EI as a combination of self-perceived, emotion-oriented personality characteristics.

Should We Teach Emotional Intelligence to Children?

If I were to answer that in one sentence, it would be: without a doubt. Everyone has different perspectives on school curriculum, but if you are being truly honest, you are probably teaching emotional intelligence to your child already. How? Certain behaviors are modeled and reinforced by observing, acknowledging, and empathizing. Even simply addressing emotional issues aids children in learning about emotions and expands their emotional vocabulary. EI aids children with understanding themselves and others, communicating, and dealing with negative emotions. It can help individuals create and maintain connections at work and in their personal lives both now and later in their lives.

Emotional Intelligence in Kids: Examples

How can we detect if our children are building emotional intelligence? Here are just a few of the countless examples:

1. They will express their feelings: Even the quietest of children will show their feelings in visible ways. While more outgoing children may be more vocal, introverted children may express themselves through a song, drawing, or even writing. These things can sometimes happen so slowly that you don't see them right away, but you will eventually start noticing them.

2. They will pay attention to others: Consider David and Sally.

David says, " I just got a dog."

Sally ignores him completely and says something totally unrelated and self-centered like, "I have a lot of homework to do."

However, after they grow up, their conversation will look something like:

David: "I just got a dog."

Sally: "Oh that's great. What's his name?" or "How big is he?"

As children grow older, they will begin to pay more attention to people and react in emotionally appropriate ways. For instance, David might tell Sally that he's enthusiastic about something his dog learned, and Jane may be delighted to hear about that.

3. They self-regulate: You may realize that a learner or child of yours is processing something emotionally at some time. It's usually a slower process in children, but it's still a significant step forward. So, if you ever witness your child take a deep breath in a situation where he would have previously responded furiously, you can acknowledge this behavior.

EI vs. IQ: Which Is More Important?

The moment we start going to school or start to get an education, we are told to focus on our grades and scores in high grade exams, among other things. As a result, we also slowly believe that IQ or intelligence quotient is the key to becoming successful in life but it's not. Sure, a higher IQ will make learning easier for a child—he will perform better in school, may win a talent hunt, or get high scores in every exam, which will give him more options to grow in the future. It's obvious that you want your child to have a high IQ quotient but a high IQ alone does not guarantee academic or life success. That's where emotional intelligence (EI) comes into picture. Even if a child has an average IQ, he can be highly motivated to work hard and face any kind of challenge. A child with an average IQ who understands when he has problems, doesn't hesitate to ask for help, and completes all his tasks on time can outperform a child with a higher IQ who is undisciplined, unmotivated, and not serious about his work.

Daniel Goleman stated that EQ may actually hold more importance than IQ. Why? Some psychologists assume that standardized intelligence measures (such as IQ scores) are too limited and do not capture the full spectrum of human intelligence (Cherry, 2013). Psychologist Howard Gardner has proposed that intelligence is more than a single general ability. Instead, he proposes that there are various intelligences and that people may excel in several of them (Cherry, 2013).

IQ was once thought to be the most important factor in determining success. Researchers questioned whether intelligence was a result of genes or the atmosphere, and people with high IQs were considered to be destined for a life of performance and success. Some opponents, however, realized that intelligence alone was not an indication of success in life. It was also possibly a too limited concept to represent the complete range of human skills and understanding. IQ is still considered a key factor in success, especially with regard to academic achievement. However, today's experts realize that IQ isn't the sole factor that determines life achievement. Instead, it's part of a larger set of factors, including emotional intelligence.

Many aspects in a child's life can influence his or her IQ, including prenatal nutrition, genetics, and how engaging the child's early atmosphere is. However, by the end of adolescence, brain growth is nearly complete, and IQ is established. EI, on the other hand, increases throughout life, culminating in the later ages and only gradually falling until our 80s. Learning EI abilities as a child is similar to learning how to tie a shoe or ride a bicycle. The ability never entirely disappears once it's learned, though it can become dull if not utilized. Since many life situations provide opportunities for children to apply their EI skills, this practice helps to solidify the skill so that it may be used even in the most difficult situations.

Parents and early childhood educators strive to produce physically, intellectually, and emotionally stable and healthy kids who can really succeed as adults. Each phase of childhood has something to do with the child's overall growth, thus it's crucial to be aware of the stages of development that a child requires. Every move and action in early childhood has a substantial impact on adulthood, according to scientific evidence. As a result, it is critical to focus on what's important—the child's current growth—while also considering the future to see what the child can gain from the current parenting and learning in early childhood.

The Mood Meter

What would a bunch of three-year-old children answer if you asked them how they are feeling? Okay? Awesome? Happy? What if you surveyed a group of early childhood educators and asked for their opinions? It's possible that their replies aren't that different! When asked how we are doing, most of us have a limited intellect to convey our feelings. On the other hand, schools that embrace children's and instructors' emotions encourage a diverse language for describing feelings. The mood meter is a tangible tool that can help people move away from rote replies like "good" and toward more complex responses like "interested," "enthusiastic," and "worried." Identifying and expressing feelings correctly allows children and adults to recognize the importance of emotions during the day. Taking time to recognize emotions, explain their sources, and brainstorm possible strategies to change or preserve them with children and adults guarantees that both adults and children use emotions successfully to foster a learning environment.

The mood meter is one of the four tools of the RULER approach. The goal of RULER is to incorporate emotional intelligence concepts into the immune system of students from preschool to grade 12, influencing leaders to lead, teachers to educate, children to learn, and families to help kids. It is somewhat similar to the talent model by Salvoey and Mayer (Yale Center, 2020). There are two axes on the mood meter. The horizontal axis symbolizes joy and ranges from -5 to +5, with -5 indicating the least enjoyable sensation you can imagine and +5 representing the happiest experience you can imagine. Our emotions are typically somewhere in the middle of these two numbers. The energy we feel in our bodies is represented by the vertical axis, which has the same range as the horizontal axis. At -5, you may feel completely exhausted of energy, whereas +5 indicates the most energy you can anticipate having in your body. The two axes combine to form four colored quadrants: red (unpleasant, higher energy), yellow (pleasant, higher energy), blue (unpleasant, lower energy), and green (pleasant, lower energy).

A simple color-only variant of the mood meter works well with young children aged three to eight. We usually describe each color with one term when first explaining the mood meter to kids: green = calm; yellow = happy; red = angry; and blue = sad. Children receive new feeling words that correlate to each color as they learn to use the mood meter. In later grades, they learn the use of numeric ranges to express their level of happiness and energy. With the help of the mood meter, children learn that feelings are not good or bad. There are some emotions that we prefer to experience more frequently than others, but all emotions are valid. Even for those negative emotions, we may learn to apply strategies that leverage the information we get from them to react in ways that make us happy.

How to Use the Mood Meter to Practice Emotional Intelligence

According to research, modeling the five RULER abilities for children is a key aspect of properly imparting emotional intelligence. One way of doing this is regularly keeping an eye on the mood meter throughout the day (Tominey et al., 2017). It is the acronym of the five emotional intelligence skills, namely recognize, understand, label, express, and regulate. This approach is typically used in schools, but you can also apply it at home with your child.

Recognize: Consider what your child is feeling right now. Our bodies can provide us clues about our levels of happiness and vitality (e.g., body language, energy level, breathing, and heart rate). Consider how the emotions may influence your child's relationships with others.

Understand: Identify why your child is feeling this way. Consider the various sources of their feelings as they fluctuate throughout the day. Identifying the sources of unpleasant feelings (e.g., people, thoughts, and events) might help us regulate and predict them so that we can respond effectively. Identifying the reasons for the emotions we want to cultivate can help us embrace them more mindfully for ourselves and others.

Label: Identify what term best characterizes your child's current state of mind. Despite the fact that the English language contains over 2,000 emotion terms, most of us utilize only a few to explain how we are feeling. We can detect our emotions properly, communicate properly, and establish appropriate regulating mechanisms by developing a strong vocabulary.

Express: Identify what is the most suitable way for your child to express what he is feeling at a particular moment and place. Each of our emotions can be expressed in a variety of ways. Some forms of emotions are more powerful than others in different situations and different settings. Explaining to youngsters what we're doing and why as we display various emotions offers them with models on how to portray their own feelings.

Regulate: Teach your child how to stop feeling a certain type of way to shift his feelings onto something else that makes him happy. What can I do to either preserve or shift my feelings? An important aspect of effective regulation is finding short-term methods for managing feelings in the moment as well as long-term approaches to handling emotions over time. Even educators who have a variety of regulation methods to choose from are more capable of managing a wide range of emotions and modeling these skills for families and children.

Chapter 5:

Emotion Coaching Through the Ages

Raising kids entails constant change. As our children mature, we adapt our lives to meet their changing needs, anxieties, interests, and abilities. Despite all of the changes, one constant remains: Each kid's desire to form an emotional bond with loving, caring adults. I'll go over five major stages of childhood in this chapter.

The Infant Stage

Who can tell when a baby's emotional connection with its parents starts? Some suggest that it originates in utero as the child reacts to its mother's various levels of anxiety or serenity. Others think it begins right after birth as families feed, comfort, and nurture their baby. Others recall a magical moment from a few weeks ago. When the infant smiles for the first time at mother or father after delivery, it brightens everyone's day. Their long hours and restless nights have finally paid off. However, most parents may say that the true fun begins around the age of three. Babies often develop interest in face-to-face social connection at the age of six months. At this age, behavioral theories refer to the infant's eyes "brightening," indicating that babies appear to be looking at their family for the first time and holding their attention. As a three-month-old infant, she is learning a great deal about how to read and show emotion through observational learning. This indicates that, even at this young age, parents can initiate an organized method of "emotion coaching" their infants through their response and attentiveness.

According to research, parents will go to tremendous measures to get and keep their newborn's attention during their early emotional interactions (Gottman et al., 2015). Most parents have face-to-face, silent "conversations" with their children, taking turns creating facial expressions. When the mother lifts her eyebrows, the baby lifts his as well. The mother and the infant both thrust out their tongues. One person coos or gurgles, and the other coos or gurgles back at the very same tone or beat. Imitation games are usually engrossing for babies, especially if the adult copies the infant in a different way. If the infant slams her rattle multiple times on the floor, the mother might mimic the beat with her voice, which her child finds fascinating. These imitative dialogues are vital because they show the infant that her parents are listening to her and reacting to his feelings. This is the baby's first sensation of being acknowledged by someone else; it's the start of emotional communication.

What happens to babies over time if their parents are unresponsive or just respond negatively? Tiffany Field, a researcher who has researched depressed women and their children, has discovered some alarming results: Sadness, low energy, limited participation, rage, and irritation are common in babies whose mothers are depressed (Gottman et al., 2015).

If a mother's depression lasts another year, her child will start to show development and growth delays in the long term. According to Field's research, the time between three and six months plays an essential role in terms of how a mother's depression affects the growth of her baby's neurological system. When Field and her team examined two groups of three-month-old newborns (one with depressed mothers and one without), they found no significant differences. However, when they examined the six-month-old newborns, they discovered that those with depressive mothers were less expressive verbally and scored lower on nervous system tests (Gottman et al., 2015).

People who aren't used to caring for babies may not realize that they require "downtime." They may continue to use toys, use baby talks, and try bouncing to excite the infant. Of course, the infant is a hostage. He is powerless to stop his demanding playmate. He is unable to leave the room. He might not even be able to hide his head under a sheet due to a lack of physical coordination and power. As a result, he must rely on his most consistent and powerful defense: crying.

My suggestion with emotion coaching is to pay close attention to and react appropriately to your infant's moods. Give your baby some time to relax if he suddenly loses interest in playing after a lot of engagement. If your baby becomes irritable in settings where he is being carried and talked to a lot, take him away to a quiet area occasionally so they can relax and rest.

The Exploration Stage: Six to Eight Months

For babies, this is an exciting time of discovery as they explore a whole new world of things, people, and destinations. Simultaneously, they're learning new methods to express and communicate emotions like delight, excitement, fear, and irritation with the people and things around them. Emotion coaching continues to expand as a result of this growing awareness. The ability of a baby to switch his focus while remembering a person or thing he is no longer gazing at is one of the significant developmental leaps that occurs around the age of six months. He used to be able to think exclusively about the person or thing he was concentrating on at the time. This achievement, as easy as it may appear, opens up a whole new world of opportunities for fun and emotional contact. He can now ask you to play with the numerous fascinating objects. He can tell you how he feels about those things.

Accept your baby's invites to play with things and mimic the baby's emotional responses to enable the growth of emotional intelligence. As a result of this, more sharing and emotional expression will emerge. By eight months, babies typically begin crawling and discovering their environment, but the explorer is also learning to distinguish differences between the various people he encounters, which sets the stage for the first significant appearance of fear. You will see this demonstrated in bouts of "stranger anxiety." A baby who once smiled indiscriminately at people in the grocery store now buried their face in the mom's shoulder. While he once leaned willingly into the waiting arms of a new babysitter, he now has formed "specific attachments" to his parents and may cling desperately when they try to set him down in a new setting with strangers around. At the same time, the baby is getting much better at understanding spoken words, which also helps with emotional communication. Although it will probably be several months before he begins to talk himself, he can understand a great deal of language and is able to follow instructions.

Physical mobility, the ability to change focus, the baby's strong connection with his parents, his knowledge of spoken language, and his fear of the unknown—all of these new traits come together in what talent psychologists describe as "social referencing." This is the baby's inclination to approach a specific object or person and then seek emotional cues from the parent. When a baby approaches an unknown dog, for example, his mother may remark, "No, don't go there!" The baby can grasp the concept of possible threat by reading the mother's advice, vocal tone, and facial expressions.

The Emotional Development Stage: Nine to 12 Months

This is the stage at which babies begin to realize that people can communicate their thoughts and feelings with one another. When a baby brings his father a broken toy, for example, he says, "Oh, it's busted—that's a pity. You're sad, aren't you?" By nine months, the infant has realized that her father understands how she feels on the inside. Previously, when a parent empathized with their child and reflected their sentiments back to them through voice inflection, facial movement, and body language, the youngster was discovering the world of emotional expression. The baby, on the other hand, was unaware that parent and child may share similar ideas and feelings.

As your child discovers the idea of "object stability," he may become enthralled by activities that let him move small things in and out of containers, hide them, and then resurface. Alternatively, he may frequently toss his spoon off his high chair or out of view, then ask you to retrieve it for him. This developing awareness of object and person constancy could be linked to another significant development in your baby's life: his increasing connection to different persons, specifically his parents. He can miss you and ask you to stay because now he knows you exist even if you're not there. When he observes you putting on your jacket or otherwise thinks that you are going out, he may make a big deal out of it.

Convince a child this age that you will come back to help him recover from the separation anxiety associated with his parents leaving. Remember that while a one-year-old may not be able to communicate properly, he often understands a lot of what you're saying, so your affirmations can be helpful. Keep in mind that he's watching for emotional signs from you, so if you act concerned or afraid about the separation, he might get it and feel the same way. As a result, it's important to find a babysitter you're familiar with, and give yourself and the baby plenty of time to get to know them before you have to leave. This will help both you and the baby feel calmer.

Finally, you may help your child practice being alone by allowing him to explore different parts of the house on his own. Allow him to crawl away to another (babyproof) area for a time before returning to watch over him. If you're in a room together and need to go to another, inform him where you will be and when you'll be back. Gradually, he'll understand that his parents can go and nothing bad will occur—he can rely on them to return when they promise they will. Keep in mind that showing your understanding of your child's thoughts and emotions will make him feel safe and emotionally connected to you.

The Toddler Stage: One to Three Years

As the child develops a feeling about himself and starts to explore his freedom, this age of toddlerhood becomes a fun and exciting time! However, there's a reason why this stage is known as the "terrible twos." It is at this age that youngsters grow more aggressive and negligent. "No!" "Mine!" "Do it by myself!" or "Me do!" are some of the most common words you'll hear while your toddler works on his linguistic skills. Emotion coaching becomes a valuable technique for parents to utilize in helping their toddlers deal with the growing irritation and rage. Parents should consider disagreements and obstacles from the child's point of view at all phases of development.

Since the toddler's major developmental job at this age is to identify himself as a self-sufficient little being, avoid problems that make him feel powerless. Conflicts between toddlers over possessions will never be totally settled. However, for your own convenience, you might want to limit such incidents. This can be accomplished by teaching children that toys should only be taken to a friend's place or a childcare center if they plan to share them. When your child has visitors coming over, have him pick a few special items that will be off the charts to the guests.

Aside from his growing knowledge of himself as distinct from others, the toddler's growing interest in symbolic and role play is a significant social development. Kids start enacting actions they've encountered in other family and friends between the ages of two and three. The skill of the child to retain memories of acts and incidents in their head and then recover them for mimicry at a later stage is remarkable. Pretending to clean, shave, clean the floor, or communicate on the phone with a two-year-old is quite entertaining. Noticing a youngster sweetly kissing his teddy bear good night or angrily scolding her dolls for behaving badly may serve as a reminder that children learn a lot about how to deal with their feelings by watching others.

The Early Childhood Stage: Four to Seven Years

By the age of four, kids are generally wandering around, making new friends, spending some time in a range of environments, and experiencing a variety of new and interesting things. New obstacles arise as a result of these experiences: School is enjoyable, but your professors will soon need you to be able to sit silently in groups and focus on the subject at hand. You normally get on well with your friends, yet they irritate you or hurt your sentiments from time to time. Now that you're mature enough to understand tragedies like home fires, battles, burglary, and death, you must guard against becoming paralyzed by fear. To master these obstacles, you'll need to be able to control your emotions, which is one of the most important developmental responsibilities for children in their early years. This means that kids must learn to control bad behavior, pay attention, and organize themselves in order to achieve an external goal.

Kids are more likely to learn emotional regulation abilities in their friendships than anywhere else. They learn how to speak clearly, share knowledge, and clarify their ideas if they are misunderstood in this setting. They learn how to communicate and play in groups. They are taught to share. Teaching children to pretend is a difficult skill to master, but once mastered, it may be put to use in a variety of ways. For example, if your child wishes he were bigger and stronger, he might remark something like, "I used to be quite little, but now I can pull at the front of the sofa." "Did you know that Superman has the ability to fly?" It's almost like the child is pleading for approval to transform into Superman in order to explore emotions of power and self-assurance. Just by saying, "Happy to see you, Superman," you can contribute to the fantasy. "Are you going to take off right now?" While performing pretend games with you, your kids may intertwine dialogues about real-life problems.

When talking to your kids about their fears, try to employ the basic principles of emotion coaching. This entails assisting children in recognizing and labeling fear when it arises, engaging with them in an empathetic manner about their anxieties, and discussing strategies for dealing with various risks. When discussing tactics for dealing with real-life threats like fire, strangers, or disease, it's also an excellent time to talk about preventive measures. "The prospect of a fire in our home is scary," you can say if your youngster exhibits a fear of fire. "That's why we have a smoke alarm on hand in case anything starts to burn." Remember that children may discuss their fears in a roundabout manner. A child who asks about the existence of orphanages is unlikely to be engaged in a lesson on child welfare policies; he is usually thinking about his own concerns of abandonment. As a result, pay attention to the sentiment behind the question, especially if they are asking about things that are upsetting to them, such as abandonment or death.

The Middle Stage: Eight to 12 Years

During this stage, kids begin to connect with a larger social group and learn social influence. They might start to observe who is in and who is out with their friends. Children are maturing mentally at the same time, discovering the strength of logic over emotion. You may notice that one of your child's key motives in life is to avoid humiliation as a result of the increasing awareness of peer pressure. Children of this age are often quite picky about the way they dress, the bags they carry, and the activities they participate in. They will go to considerable measures to avoid drawing attention to themselves, particularly if it would result in mocking or criticism from their friends. While this may upset parents who really want their kids to be leaders rather than followers, conformity is beneficial at this stage. It indicates that your child is improving his ability to read social signs, a skill that will be useful throughout his life. It's especially crucial in early adolescence because youngsters this age can be cruel in their bullying and humiliation. Indeed, at this stage, mocking is the forge that shapes many ethical standards.

Girls and boys both tease one another, while boys' teasing can sometimes lead to physical violence. Since the stakes are so high, children learn quickly that the best way to respond to teasing is to display no feelings at all. If you turn your way around, you'll have a fair chance of keeping your honor. Children of this age are growing increasingly conscious of the power of intelligence while simultaneously attempting to suppress their emotions. Many people see a significant improvement in their ability to think rationally around the age of 10. They take pleasure in reacting to the environment as if their brains were computers. If you ask a nine-year-old to pick up their socks, they might raise each one and then set it in its proper location, saying, "You didn't instruct me to pick them up." Such an attitude and mockery of the grown-up world are expected from a child who sees reality in either/or terms.

If you discover that your child is involved in a mistreatment of another child that you believe is unjust, express your displeasure to them. Use it as a chance to express your principles of fairness and kindness. However, unless the conduct was absolutely malicious, I would suggest against a severe reaction or penalty. Peer pressure are typical behaviors for youngsters of this age. You can use emotion coaching approaches to assist your child in coping with emotions of grief and frustration if he complains of being ignored or mistreated by peers. Then, assist him in coming up with solutions to these problems. When it comes to children mocking adult customs, I advise parents not to take their children's comments too seriously. Middle childhood is characterized by sass, mockery, and a disregard for adult ideals. However, if you truly believe your child has been rude to you, tell him just how you feel. ("I get the impression that you don't respect me when you laugh at my dressing style.") This is another technique to instill values in the household, such as compassion and mutual understanding. As always, kids of this age require emotional connection with their parents as well as the caring supervision that such a connection provides.

The Adolescent Stage

The teenage years are a time where kids are most concerned about their identity and ask themselves questions like, "Who am I? Who should I be? Am I becoming the right person?" As a result, don't be startled if your adolescent appears to become completely self-absorbed at some point. His involvement in family problems will decrease as his friendships become more important. After all, it is only through his friends that he will learn who he is beyond the protection of his family. Despite this, a teenager's concentration is generally on himself, even within his social interactions. Teens are on a path of self-realization, and they are continuously maneuvering, first in one way, then in another, in search of the right path. They try out new personalities, new worlds, and new facets of themselves. This kind of exploration among adolescents is beneficial. Their path, on the other hand, is not always easy. Hormonal fluctuations might cause mood swings that are out of control. Unpleasant forces in the social environment may take advantage of young people's fragility, placing them at risk for issues such as drugs, assault, and unsafe sexual conduct. Exploration, on the other hand, tends to be a fundamental and inevitable element of human growth.

Teens tend to be the most likely to experience such choices regarding their sexuality and self-acceptance. A female develops a sexual attraction to a boy she doesn't like. ("He's very adorable, but of course he has to speak up and spoil everything.") A little boy finds himself expressing beliefs that he formerly objected to in his father. ("I can't believe what I'm hearing! I sound exactly like my father!") The adolescent suddenly understands that life isn't all that black and white—it's made up of various shades of gray. Whether the teen likes it or not, all of those colors may indeed be found within him. Being a parent of a teen is just as challenging as finding one's way through adolescence.

Remember that adolescence marks the beginning of a child's separation from his or her parents. Parents must realize that teenagers require privacy. Listening in on your son's chats, reading his notebook, or interrogating him too much sends the signal that you don't believe him. This, in turn, creates a communication barrier. During challenging times, your child may come to perceive you as an opponent instead of an ally. You must acknowledge a child's right to be uncomfortable and dissatisfied at times, in addition to his privacy. If your teen openly shares his emotions to you, don't act as if you immediately understand. Teenagers often believe that their achievements are unique due to their fresh outlook. When adults find their actions apparent and their reasons obvious, they feel humiliated. As a result, take your time talking and listen to your child with an unbiased view. Don't assume you've heard and understood anything he's said. Since adolescence is a phase of individuation, be aware that your teenager may choose clothing trends, hairstyles, songs, paintings, and language that you dislike. Remember that you don't have to agree with your child's choices—all you have to do is accept them.

Similarly, don't strive to mimic your adolescent's choices. Allow his clothing, music, actions, and language. Show respect for your adolescent. Consider what it would feel to be treated by your best friend in the same way that many parents treat their kids. How would it feel if you were continuously being corrected, notified of your flaws, or teased about personal issues? What if your friend gave you endless lectures, instructing you what to do about your life in a judgmental tone? You'd probably get the impression that this person didn't care about your feelings and didn't respect you.

While I won't suggest that parents should treat their adolescents like friends (the parent-child relation is significantly more complicated), I will say that teenagers need the same level of respect as our peers. As a result, I would advise you to refrain from mocking, criticizing, or humiliating. Express your views to your child, but do so in a nonjudgmental and concise manner. Nobody enjoys being preached at, especially teens. Don't use characteristic labels (lazy, selfish, careless, or greedy) to talk about your teen's behavior when you have a disagreement. Instead, speak in terms of specific behaviors, explaining to your child how her actions influence you.

Chapter 6:

Cognitive Scaffolding

Cognitive scaffolding is a method of learning where assistance is offered in order to support learning. Like the scaffolding on the side of a building under construction, the assistance offered is usually a sort of boost to help the learner master their task or concept, and in no way is this a permanent solution. Once the learner has grasped the new concept or mastered the new task, the assistance will no longer be required, like the scaffolding around a construction site is removed after the job is done. The most important aspect of cognitive scaffolding is allowing the child, or learner, to complete as much of the task or understand as much of the concept as possible unassisted. Assistance should only be offered on tasks that are beyond the child's capabilities (West et al., 2017).

Lev Vygotsky, a Russian psychologist who has done extensive research on child psychology and development, believed that a learner's developmental level consists of two parts: the actual developmental level and the potential developmental level. Vygotsky then went further to describe the Zone of Proximal Development (ZPD) as "the distance between the actual development level as determined through problem solving and the level of potential development as determined through problem solving under adult guidance" (Fisher & Frey, 2010).

Basically, the Zone of Proximal Development is the difference between what a learner can accomplish independently and what can be accomplished with the help of a more knowledgeable individual. By the more knowledgeable other sharing knowledge with the said learner, the gap between what is known and what is unknown is bridged (West et al., 2017).

The actual term "scaffolding," however, came from Wood, Bruner, and Ross (1976) who described the term as a process to enable an individual to achieve a goal that would be beyond their efforts had they not been offered assistance.

According to *Instructional-Design Theories and Models: A New Paradigm of Instructional Theory* by Charles Reigeluth (1999), there are four different kinds of scaffolding:

1. Conceptual

2. Metacognitive

3. Procedural

4. Strategic

Let's have a look at them one by one.

Conceptual Scaffolding

Conceptual scaffolding guides learners and gives them a direction as to what to think about during the learning process. If learners are having problems understanding course content, they may become discouraged and lose motivation. Conceptual scaffolding helps learners benefit while they engage with such challenging subjects by assisting them in identifying crucial theoretical concepts and organizing them into meaningful frameworks that promote learning. This strategy includes advanced organizers, graphics organizers, and outlines. In 1960, David Ausubel, an American psychologist, recommended the use of advance organizers in his journal known as *Journal of Educational Psychology* (Blended Learning, 2011). Advanced organizers assist learners to connect previous knowledge with the latest information. For example, it could be by providing the summary of the key points in a reading passage and describing content in a more abstract, generic, and inclusive manner. It differs from a summary in that it connects information to learners' present cognitive structure, enhancing existing knowledge and allowing them to connect old learning to new ideas.

Learners use previous knowledge to understand the meaning of new information presented to them.

Metacognitive Scaffolding

Metacognitive scaffolding helps learners build thinking skills to support their learning. Learners who have never attended any classes, have been away from school for a long time, or who have never acquired solid cognitive skills would benefit from scaffolding while they participate in the learning activities. Learners with less developed cognitive skills have a harder time learning, making them more likely to drop out. Metacognitive scaffolding helps learners organize, analyze, and evaluate their learning practices to make sure they are processing knowledge effectively and efficiently for storage and recall. As learners become more conscious of their thinking, they can utilize this awareness and improve their learning. Metacognitive learning strategies involve tracking information and making sure if the learners are on the right track and working toward the correct goals, plus the prospective results of their efforts. There are a variety of scaffolding strategies that can be learned to keep track of their progress. Study guides and workbooks are useful tools for students to keep track of their progress. These tools can help students focus on the parts of a work as well as the sequence in which they should be performed.

Procedural Scaffolding

Procedural scaffolding particularly works in the online learning process. Procedural scaffolding assists learners how to navigate their classrooms and participate in learning activities. Learners can find it hard to understand what they have to do when they start an online course. This difficulty is exacerbated by a lack of a standard system template when the online program is built because students need to focus on a new navigational structure and position of classes for every new online course. They must also discover how the content is presented, how the study units are organized, what the expectations for the content are, and other distinctive features. Procedural tutoring can help students to continue learning through orientation toward the course; assist them in understanding the expectations for involvement; and to recognize processes, tools, and resources that will be used throughout the curriculum.

Strategic Scaffolding

Strategic scaffolding provides training to help individual learners understand learning preferences and previous knowledge to help them achieve what they are looking for. Cognitive overload can be a problem for novice learners, so the practices aimed at simplifying the content and organizing data into discrete sections help students to process information more easily. Alternative explanations can help students better understand the concepts by making them see other ways to look at the ideas that are presented. Learners sometimes might need hints or examples in order to fully understand the next step or activities and get a basic framework for the next phase of a given activity. Worked examples can also help learners by offering them a way of thinking about a problem-solving process. The key is to deliver well-worked examples that allow learners to get a general idea to work on new issues. Additional resources can also help learners to develop a learning task strategically by fostering skill and expertise gaps.

Cognitive scaffolding is a way to assist children in the gap between what they can achieve themselves and what they can achieve with the help of someone with more extensive knowledge, skills, and/or tools that help them work independently without any need of someone else. The key is to introduce cognitive scaffolding strategies in the right amount. According to Nada Dabbagh, professor and director of the Division of Learning Technologies at George Mason University writes the following:

> . . . too much scaffolding could result in dampening learners' efforts to actively pursue their learning goals, causing them to lose their momentum or drive toward meaning making and self-directed learning efforts, and too little scaffolding could result in students' inability to successfully complete or perform

certain tasks and instructional activities, leading to anxiety, frustration, and finally loss of motivation and attrition. (Blended Learning, 2011)

In the process of cognitive scaffolding to help you raise an emotionally intelligent child, you, the parent, are the more knowledgeable individual whose assistance is required.

There are three areas of the brain that are involved in learning a new skill: the prefrontal cortex, the parietal cortex, and the cerebellum. As a task or skill is mastered after consistent practice, these areas become less involved and take up less cognitive energy and focus. This allows there to be more focus and energy on new skills as the learned skill becomes somewhat habitual. Cognitive support and scaffolding can be applied when a child is having difficulty achieving a goal and seems to be using large amounts of focus and cognitive energy. The temporary assistance and support can make learning the skill more efficient and timeous and allow more focus and cognitive energy to be available to the child for other activities (Fisher & Frey, 2010). The child will eventually self-regulate and become independent in their skills.

Scaffolding can be done in more than one way to aid in child development such as:

- Breaking the task into smaller parts

- Verbalizing thinking processes

- Cooperative learning

- Prompts

- Questioning to allow the child to draw their own conclusions

- Cue cards

- Giving tips

- Providing strategies

- Providing knowledge and information

It is important to know a child's abilities and skills before deciding which method of scaffolding would work best.

In order for children to learn, they need to interact with others who are more intelligent than they currently are in order to attain the skills that the more intelligent individual already possesses. For example, when a child is learning how to walk, they hold on to the legs or pants of their parents and hold themselves up until they are proficient in the skill. Learning how to walk this way is much more efficient than walking without aid or observing others who can walk (Sarikas, 2018).

It's very important to understand the difference between cognitive scaffolding and assisting your child in their growth and development versus helping your child to point that they become passive learners, and their growth is hindered. This can be prevented by simply observing before jumping in to help. Allow the child to attempt to learn the skill or grasp the concept before deciding that they need your help.

Here are a few cognitive scaffolding tips that you can practice with your child.

1. Seeing Is Believing

When trying to break down a concept to help your child understand a bit better, use visual representations and physical props. When looking at the concept of emotional intelligence remember that your child's brain is not yet fully developed to understand each emotion. Often, being unable to express what they are feeling leads to more irritability and confusion in children. When talking about feelings, try showing them pictures of people who are angry or irritable, and ask if that's what they're feeling; you can even make different faces to try to show how you are feeling in the moment. When trying to explain other more abstract concepts as well, use visual aids and point to certain pictures while asking questions so that the child may arrive at the answer themselves.

2. Talk It Out

Since children do not have the vocabulary and knowledge that adults have about the world around us, they find it difficult to express themselves. Sometimes, they get so stuck and irritated that you are not able to understand them, which can often lead to temper tantrums and shouting. First, acknowledge your child's feelings, reassuring them that you understand why they're frustrated, and then explain that you are going to get through this together. Allow your child to express themselves with whatever words they know. As they talk, teach them new words that you feel relate to the situation. This will help build their vocabulary, cognitive abilities, as well emotional intelligence.

If your child is struggling with a math or comprehension problem while doing their homework, and you can sense a tantrum coming on, you are going to want to take a deep breath in and simply say, "Let's talk it out." Thinking aloud or talking out a child's issue allows them to identify the errors in their own thinking more easily. If they're unable to see their errors, prompt them by drawing attention to what they're saying.

Let's look at an example. Your six-year-old little girl is sitting at the dining room table and doing some homework that her kindergarten teacher has given her. She's practicing copying down words for a spelling test on Friday. After a while you hear your little girl let out a long sigh and just begin to cry. When you ask her what happened, she says that she doesn't know what the last word on the list is. You take a look at the list, and the last word is "game." The other words in the list are fairly simple, and it's obvious that the teacher added that last one to separate the men from the boys. Well, your little girl is going to get this! You sit down next to hear and tell her that you know she can do this. You ask her to think and spell the word out loud. She says each letter out loud through her muffled tears. Then you ask her what she thinks that spells. She replies that it spells "gammie" but she knows that it's not a real word and the teacher told her that the spelling list was all about things they did at school. She breaks down crying again and you tell her to sound out the letters. When she gets to the letter "a," you explain that sometimes it can be pronounced a little differently, and when it's pronounced that way, then the letter "e" at the end isn't pronounced at all. Then you ask her what she thinks the word is now. You see a light in her eyes as she currently pronounces the word "game" and wipes away her tears as she leans in for a hug. You have just created a new neural pathway and enhanced your little girl's cognitive ability. Wait until she sees the word "same" on a page! She'll be ready!

3. Ask Questions

Rather than just teaching your child what you know, ask them questions so that they can come up with the answer by themselves. This builds confidence and problem-solving skills. Also, don't discourage the child by blatantly claiming that their views or thoughts are wrong, rather mention that not many people see it that way or in some other kind way.

For example, if your 13-year-old son is struggling with the concept of gravity, it's time to talk it out. Ask him what he thinks gravity is and how he would explain it. If he says he doesn't know, then tell him to take a wild guess. Let's say he says that it's what keeps us on the ground. He's right! Ask him what he doesn't understand, since it seems like he knows what gravity is about. Let's say he doesn't understand how planes are able to fly if gravity is pulling us down. Now it's time to ask some questions so that he can draw his own conclusions and feel curious to look into it further. Ask questions like, "Have you ever seen a bird fly?" "Have you ever heard of aerodynamics?" "Remember when we went parasailing last summer?" These will help with overall conversation.

4. The Three-Solution Rule

Often, if cognitive scaffolding is not practiced right, a child becomes dependent on an adult and cognitively lazy. In order to prevent this, teach your child that if he/she comes across any type of problem, while learning or otherwise, they should think of and carry out at least three solutions before coming to you and claiming that they just cannot do it.

For example, if your seven-year-old daughter simply cannot fit her lunchbox in her bag, she needs to try at least three solutions before she comes to you to ask for a bigger schoolbag. She can try changing her lunchbox to a smaller one from the cupboard, using a lunch bag instead, or even carrying her lunch in another smaller bag altogether. If these solutions have been proven not to work, only then should she come to you with the problem. Once again, this teaches-problem solving skills and independence.

Chapter 7:

Where's the Discipline in That?

So, you are at the grocery store grabbing some essentials before heading home to cook. You are walking down the baking aisle with your kid in tow, and she stops in front of the baking utensils. She grabs a baking tray and puts it into the shopping cart, then holds your hand and continues to walk on. You stop what you are doing and squat down so that you are on the same level as her. You then calmly explain that you have that exact baking tray at home, and you can show her where it is when you get home. Then you put the tray back on the shelf and reach for her hand again. She tugs away and starts to cry. You try your best to calm her down, but she isn't hearing anything from her new archenemy—you did put back the baking tray, after all. She's wailing in the middle of the aisle, and you lose your cool and shout at her. Now you are in a bad mood, she's in a bad mood, and you are pretty sure the guy who was packing the next aisle might have thought that you kidnapped the kid from somewhere. What I just described is every parent's worst nightmare: A child that acts out in public. If we were the child in that situation, one look from our parents would cause every cell in our body to freeze! Heck, we wouldn't have even had the audacity to put anything into the cart. That feeling of utter fear from disobedience wasn't from a place of having good healthy discipline or being a well-mannered child. It was simply the authority that our parents had in our lives.

I'm sure we all want well-behaved children who remember to use their manners and give up their seat to the elderly and pregnant, but this isn't going to just develop overnight. Discipline teaches a child that every action has a reaction, and every choice comes with consequences. If good actions are carried out and good choices are made, then the reaction and consequences are good as a result. While learning the idea of action and reaction or choice and consequence, your child will learn to take responsibility for their own actions and choices.

Accountability is something that needs to be instilled into a child at an early age. The concept of accountability is often lost as children grow; to prevent this, they need to be reminded of it constantly. The aim of discipline and accountability is ultimately to encourage a child to manage their behavior, and when it comes to emotional intelligence, manage their emotions as well. Children take action and make choices based on their emotions because the part of their brain that is associated with emotion is usually developed by the time the child is very young. Emotion comes pretty naturally. Intellect and logic, on the other hand, are developed at a slower pace and depend on what the child is exposed to in their external environment. A child who listens to bedtime stories every night, for example, will improve their linguistic intelligence, and their comprehension levels will be superior to a child who does not. A child who listens to classical music while engaging in their normal activities will be able to perceive changes in pitch and tone more easily and will be able to remember melodies, thus improving their memory.

Remember, even though you might consider your child a mini adult, they do not have the emotional, mental, or physical abilities of an adult just yet. These need to be developed, and you need to help them develop. Just like adults, however, a child's actions and choices are largely dependent on their emotions and state of mood. This means that emotional intelligence is the key to discipline as well.

In the situation described at the beginning of the chapter, one of the questions that would have been important to ask the child is, "Why do you want the baking pan?" Understanding the reasons behind why your child behaves a certain way is important. Maybe your child has taken a new liking to a TV show about baking, and she wants to be a baker. Remember, your child's interests will change as they grow, but taking an interest in their interests is a good way to build a relationship.

Parenting has changed drastically over the years, and the new explosion in the world of technology and the general globalization simply means that you are no longer the only influence in your child's life. Mischief and misbehavior are portrayed as funny and charming in TV shows, and defiance against authority is somewhat advertised as the only path to liberation. The teenage years are sometimes unbearable for parents, who find it difficult to get their point across and help their child see that they only want the best for them. That's why the first few years of a child's life are so important as well as the ability to adapt as a parent.

Instilling structure, discipline, and an understanding of accountability in the early years of child development will lay the foundation and help your child make choices that are in their best interest, as well as those that are in keeping with their values. It is important to understand, however, that your child will not always have the same values as you. Although the love and care that you have brought them up with will provide a set of core values, some values of theirs might differ from yours, and you need to be mindful of this. Your child might still value honesty, kindness, and strive for excellence, like you taught them, but they might also value good humor, environmentalism, and animal rights—a set of ideas that you have never really subscribed to.

The number one reason that children act out or misbehave is that they crave attention, and sometimes they're so starved of attention that even the bad kind will do. The other reason that children misbehave is that they don't understand their emotions, so their irritability at being unable to properly express themselves comes out in anger and tantrums.

Discipline, by definition, is the practice of training people to obey rules or a code of behavior, using punishment to correct disobedience (Oxford Dictionary, 2018). Some parents choose to practice the negative kind of discipline by instilling a fear into the child in order to punish disobedience. This might be the fear of a sound beating, the fear of manual labor or even, in some extreme cases, the fear of being sent to bed hungry. These methods have shown to be counterproductive in the long term and lead to difficult parent-child relationships. Don't get me wrong, I'm not saying pat your kid on the back every time they talk back to you; What I'm saying is that maybe you don't need to deny them the basic human need of food. There are better ways to discipline a child.

The rules or code of behavior included in the definition above usually refers to an unspoken understanding of what is acceptable and not acceptable and comes from a general understanding of right and wrong. Even though there isn't a book of rules for life, we all have the general understanding that stealing is wrong, and helping out someone in need is right. As a parent, when you begin teaching your child the difference between right and wrong, you go according to a "rule book" that you have compiled by thinking about things like what you want your child to learn, how you want your child to act, what you loved about your childhood, what you hated about your childhood, etc. Every single person on this planet has a different rule book based on their own personal experiences in life. Although your rule book has a couple chapters on socially acceptable behavior, your chapter 11 might be about how you want your child to grow up earning an allowance to teach them the value of money. On the contrary, your best friend's chapter 11 might be about giving their child every desire so they are never left wanting, like she and her sisters were when they grew up in poverty. Both these ideas, although positive and intended with the best of intentions, also have the potential to have negative effects on the child as they grow, so it's important to balance out all ideas if possible. Your child could grow up with the idea that money makes one happy, while your best friend's child could grow up with a sense of entitlement. This is where discipline comes in.

Why Discipline Matters

You see, many people misunderstand what discipline means. Discipline means that you want your child to live the happiest life possible, and from your personal experiences and the unspoken rules of society, you have an idea of what skills your child needs to develop in order to be happy, successful, and live a good life. Of course, you understand that your ideas of what's best for your child is limited to your experiences, but once your child is old enough to make their own decisions, you would have equipped him/her with all the skills necessary to make the decision that is in their best interest and in keeping with their values.

For the end goal to be happiness and success, you need to train your child to adhere to the rules you set so that they can learn all that they need in order to become functional members of society.

The healthy meaning of the verb form of discipline is "to teach"—which is something that can be done in a variety of ways that are supportive and that promote the development of increasingly empathetic and ethical behavior in our child. The ways that we discipline our children—the ways we teach them—directly impact whether or not they develop healthy self-discipline.

When your child screams and cries in public because you can't afford to buy them the toy that they want, you are not punishing them because you are embarrassed by their behavior; you are punishing them because they need to learn that demanding for something is not how to achieve anything in life. They need to learn to be grateful for what they have before demanding something more. They need to learn that instant gratification is not healthy, and working and waiting for something has more value. They need to learn patience and lose their entitlement. These are all skills that they need to develop in order to become functional and honorable members of society. Remember, the word "punish" has come to have such negative connotations, but in reality, it's simply laying a penalty for going against the rules.

Proverbs 13:24 says, "He that spareth his rod hateth his son: but he that loveth he chasteneth him betimes" (*King James Bible*, 1611/2013).

You don't punish your children because you wish to cause them harm, you punish them because you love them so much that you want them to be happy. Since they are young and have little experience in the art of living, you are the one who knows best. You want them to be the best versions of themselves possible, so you push them.

Proverbs 23:13 says, "Withhold not correction from the child: for if thou beatest him with the rod, he shall not die" (*King James Version Bible*, 1611/2013).

Trust yourselves as parents to know what is best for your child. Your discipline is not intended to harm your child in any way; if anything, it aims to make them better versions of themselves. It's your job as a parent to teach your child what he/she needs to learn in order to thrive.

Positive disciplining involves a set of rules and regulations where communication and understanding are the foundation. This discipline doesn't seem enforced and helps build a relationship with trust and empathy, but hear me when I say it's not all rainbows and sunshine. Practicing positive discipline requires patience and perseverance and is much more difficult than it may seem. It's relatively easy and somewhat second nature to us to say things like, "You talk back to me one more time and you will be washing the dishes for two weeks straight," but once again, these disciplinary techniques are instilling fear and can cause an excess amount of resentment. Positive discipline might have you saying, "That's the second time you've talked back to me today; is something bothering you?" However, this comes with the additional difficulties of maintaining your authority while still admitting now and again that you are also a work in progress.

Good discipline comes from being your child's parent before being their friend and is not always easy when you feel like you are hurting your child's feelings. Nobody said parenting was going to be easy! Many parents have reported feeling worse than their kids when they have to discipline them. The way you can keep yourself in check is to remind yourself why you are saying what you are saying or doing what you are doing. You are saying "NO" because your child has to learn that nothing in life comes easy. You are responsible for motivating, developing, training, and building their confidence. They need to understand what is acceptable and what is not. They need to know which actions will reap rewards and which will bring chaos.

Chapter 8:

Positive Discipline

Positive parenting or discipline refers to a method of discipline that focuses on guiding and teaching children about acceptable behaviors using positive and uplifting means. While this form of discipline has shown to have positive outcomes—children who are brought up by parents using this method have shown to become successful parents themselves—it's important to foster a relationship with your children while still maintaining boundaries and the household hierarchy. You are a parent before you are a friend, and as much as discipline may leave you feeling bad, remember the reason behind the actions you take when it comes to your kids.

Positive discipline focuses on the relationship between the parent and child and is based on open communication. It helps develop a child's understanding and improve intellectual abilities as well as problem-solving skills. The most important part of positive discipline is that it focuses on the emotional well-being of the child as well and significantly contributes to emotional intelligence.

There are many advantages of positive discipline (Jarvis & Roffe, 2020, p. 102):

- It teaches children self-discipline.

- It teaches children responsibility and accountability.

- It improves problem-solving skills.

- It develops a sense of respect between parent and child.

- It improves children's self-confidence.

- It develops children's emotional intelligence.

Tips and Tricks to Positive Discipline

Below are some ideas to keep in mind when practicing positive discipline (Morin, 2021):

Redirection

During the first few years of life, children often have a short attention span, so redirecting them to another activity or drawing their attention toward something else when they're acting out is really quite easy.

With older children, redirection is a little more difficult. Saying "Do not hit your sister!" will just make them want to hit their sister even more. Saying, "You can't watch any more TV today!" will definitely lead to a tantrum. Try telling your children what they can and are allowed to do rather than what they can't and aren't allowed to. Rather than saying that they cannot watch TV, say, "Now, we can either start a new puzzle or do some coloring—your choice." Giving them a choice also gives them that sense of autonomy that children crave.

Get to the Bottom of It!

Remember when I described that shopping scene where your daughter was distraught because you wouldn't buy the baking tray because you had an identical one at home? Her reaction to you not getting the baking pan might seem a little overdramatic to the average adult, but you have to remember, during the first few years of life, the various parts of your child's brain are still in the process of developing. Although the emotions in her brain might be completely functional, her linguistic and comprehension skills are still at a low, so she doesn't know how to understand and express what she's feeling yet. You as the parent, however, with your better developed comprehension and linguistic skills, need to use these skills in order to get to the source of the problem. You need to understand why your child is acting the way he/she is, and in the process, teach them ways in which they can deal with what they're feeling in a healthy way.

Instead of immediately responding by shouting at your child or instilling the fear of manual labor, talk the situation through by describing exactly what happened and then following the description with questions.

Let's take an example. Let's say you are at a friend's house and your five-year-old son is playing with your friend's child's toy robot. Then, the boy decides that he wants to play with the robot, so he grabs it from your son's hand. In response to this, your son kicks him in the shin and then proceeds to cry, although he was not physically hurt. You would start out by asking your son exactly what happened. Once he's explained the situation to you, repeat it so that he can confirm or deny what you understand from what he told you. While describing the incident, include negative phrases to place importance on things that you want your son to focus on as well. For example, you may say, "So Jason pulled the robot out of your hand, but he didn't hurt you in any way." While you are saying these phrases, make physical contact, and make sure that your son is making eye contact with you, even if you have to gently tilt his chin up to bring his gaze to yours. Try not to exhibit any anger.

Once you understand what happened, ask questions to try to identify what was the cause of the problem. In the above situation, you might ask:

- What made you want to kick Jason?

- Have you ever kicked anyone before?

- Has Jason ever hurt you before?

- Has Jason ever hurt anyone before?

- Has Jason ever been mean to you before?

- Have you ever been mean before?

- Why did you cry even though you weren't hurt?

Now, the questions above seem pretty emotionless and matter-of-fact, but remember, when you are asking the questions, it's important to show that you are not angry, and you just want to understand—it's okay to tell your child that as well.

Let's say, in the above situation, your son was just angry that Jason grabbed the robot that he enjoyed playing with. He didn't know how to channel that anger, so he acted on instinct and kicked the boy in the shin.

Once you have established the root of the problem, it's time to reinforce a sense of discipline.

First, you can start by asking more questions to help your child draw his/her own conclusions. You may want to ask questions like:

- How did you feel when Jason grabbed the toy?

- Do you think what you did was the right thing to do?

- How do you think you would have liked to be treated if you were in Jason's position?

- Do you still want to be friends with Jason?

- You must have hurt Jason pretty badly if he was crying like that. What do you think is the right thing to do now?

You can use the opportunity to teach your child a couple of life lessons. In the above example, you might want to talk about anger and how it can sometimes get the better of us, the importance of talking about your emotions before acting, not causing pain to others, and other similar things. Also, reinforce the fact that you will always be on your child's side and love them no matter what. Remind them that they can always come to you, and you will always try to understand before reacting.

Communicate, Communicate, Communicate

There is no such thing as too much communication when it comes to parenting! As a parent, your role is often to listen to what your child has to say, ask questions to prompt their understanding and help them draw their own conclusions, and provide alternate ways to look at things to expand the way your child thinks.

Once again, when dealing with very young children, it's important to remember that they often become irritable because they find it difficult to express themselves. Relate the current situation to other situations that you observed to be similar. For example, if your child is a little quiet while you are out for a walk in the park and you find them clinging to you, ask them how they are feeling. You might ask, "Are you feeling scared like that time Daddy took you to the beach, and you saw that big dog? Are you feeling shy like that time when we visited Mommy's friend at her house? Are you feeling tired like that time we went to Grandma's house when it was already dark outside?" You should always question any changes in behavior that you observe in a child.

Praise Good Behavior

. . . but don't overdo it! Don't let good behavior go unappreciated, but don't promise a reward for every little thing. Mentioning your child's good actions and taking some time to mention how proud you are of them is great. This will keep them motivated to do better. Keep rewards for big occasions. Don't create the expectation that there's always a prize on the other side of the door, waiting for when your child comes home after holding the door open for an elderly woman or taking the initiative to clean after themselves. Showing appreciation with compliments and singing their praises is the best thing to do!

Embrace Failures With Them

Failures are not failures if you learn from them! Make sure that your child knows that there is no such thing as failure except for failure to try. Always let them know that there is nothing to be ashamed about if they tried and didn't succeed with the first attempt. Each time they fail, they learn something new, and that's the way of life. Try to build your child's self-confidence and self-belief; motivate them as much as possible while still being realistic about their abilities. If your child is not good at soccer, then maybe try another sport. If your kid can't run a mile, then maybe he's not meant to be on the track team.

No Arguments

Many parents feel like allowing their child to argue or get their point across while yelling at the top of their lungs is a good way for them to let off some steam and express themselves. This is not true. Condoning a screaming match between you and your child is counterproductive and shifts the dynamic of the family hierarchy. Engaging in arguments with your child somewhat decreases your authority in the household. It's important not to let your child's outrage and argumentative tone catch you off guard or overwhelm you, especially when they're going through those teenage years where their linguistic and comprehensive abilities are now highly developed, and they seem to want to get a word in wherever they can. Always acknowledge your child's feelings, and try to predict where you think the conversation is going. It is very important that during any sort of argument, neither party makes any personal remarks about the other's character or hurtful comments pertaining to a situation in which the other party was left to feel embarrassed, hurt, guilty, or any other feelings that could affect self-image and self-belief. It's important that this line is not crossed and that communication is civilized, even if it means taking a time-out and coming back together when both parties have had time to think.

Reduce Alone Time

When your child is acting out or after some bad behavior, don't allow them to shut themselves in their rooms or spend too much time alone. "Time-outs" are also particularly ineffective. Alone time while experiencing emotions that are difficult to express can cause more irritation for a child. Sitting alone and constantly thinking, stewing on those thoughts and emotions, end up doing worse than good. Rather, interact with your child by playing a board game together, unpacking their feelings, or even just sitting and chatting.

Use Single-Word Reminders

Instead of constantly nagging or going on long rants, use small but impactful words to get your message across in the moment. Use direct instructions in the moment like saying "kitchen" instead of explaining that you asked them to clean the kitchen and take out the trash 10 times already. When you are sure that your child has heard you, don't repeat yourself again. Constant repetition leads to the bad habit of waiting for a follow-up directive before acting, among children (Morin, 2021).

Chapter 9:

More Healthy Discipline

Sometimes, as long as you can calmly communicate with your child and explain the difference between right and wrong, or why throwing sand at their brother's head is not a good idea, children will not listen. Those little things have a mind of their own, and sometimes they will not obey the rules. You will find that this sense of rebellion grows as time goes by, and by the teenage years, you have almost no say in their actions and choices. While trusting that you have instilled the right values in them is a good way to go, once again, it's important to remember that you are no longer the only influence in your child's life.

You see, children have this habit of looking at their friends' lives and seeing castles, rainbows, and unicorns, then looking at their own lives and seeing dungeons, mud, and moss. Unfortunately, it's human nature to want what others have and not be content with your own life. I mean, all you mothers out there, don't you read those magazines about famous actresses and wish you had their skin and hair? All you fathers out there, don't you watch a fancy car drive past you on the highway and wish it was you in that Porsche? It's human nature to want more than we have, but always looking at what others do and not feeling content in your own life is a recipe for disaster. It's bound to lead to poor mental health, constant searching for something better, and finding it difficult to be happy. That's why teaching children gratitude and acceptance is a vital part of laying the foundation for a happy and healthy life for them.

I'm sure if you have a teenager at home, you sometimes watch them and wonder where all the time went. It seems like only yesterday they were in diapers, and you were their whole world. They were such well-behaved toddlers who would listen to you, and you felt like you really had the parenting thing under control at that point. Then, they start high school, and you begin to see changes in attitude; they no longer listen to what you tell them, they think they know best, and they're all unpleasant to be around sometimes. You start to wonder exactly where you went wrong and what you could have done differently. STOP BLAMING YOURSELF!

Parenting is no walk in the park! you are doing the best you can, and you are not a horrible person if sometimes you just don't have the patience to deal with your daughter's whining or your son's newfound attitude. Cut yourself some slack. Like I said, you are no longer the only influence in your child's life anymore. You could have done everything right, raised a well-behaved darling who never forgets their manners and is always mindful of others, and they can still come home from school and refuse to talk to you about their day.

Have you ever seen moss growing on the side of a house or one of those houses that need to be painted? After a fresh coat of paint, the house looks stunning—like something out of one of those home design magazines. The house is constantly exposed to the elements, but it never crumbles or falls; its foundation is sturdy and rigid. After a couple days of rain, you see a little bit of moss growing on the bottom of one of the walls. Soon the moss spreads until the bottom half of the wall is completely covered. You feel down and out because you just spent all that time and effort into making it look so beautiful with that new coat of paint, and now, here's this moss that seems to be taking away from your hard work. Still, the house is sturdy. Its foundations are strong, and it won't cave in. Then, there's a whole two weeks of sunshine and clear skies. The moss begins to fade away because it needs the moisture of the rain to flourish. Now, the paint on the wall is cracking and peeling off. Still, the foundations are strong, and the walls will not fall. You see, the appearance of the house changed constantly, but the foundations never faltered. Your job as a parent is to develop your child's foundation so that they are strong and sturdy, and while the appearance of the house might change, you need to find peace in the fact that the foundation will not. When your child is going through their rebellious phase or the phase where everything you say is wrong, remember, the appearance may change, but the foundations are sturdy.

Just like the house is exposed to the elements and the appearance changes as the weather does, the people in your child's life will influence their actions as well. If your child is the house, his/her friends are the elements, and their actions and choices are the appearance of the house. When your child strays too far off the path of virtue and their values, however, you need to be able to identify it and help them find their path again. During this time, the foundations might start to get a bit shaky, and this usually happens after a big experience or many little experiences that build up. In the house analogy, an earthquake can disrupt the foundations immediately but so can plumbing leaks, slowly and over a long period of time. Okay, enough of the metaphor, let's get into some more healthy discipline.

When your child is straying too far off the path and they refuse to communicate with you, some other healthy discipline techniques can steer them back. Remember, healthy discipline is about teaching and guiding children so that they can develop all the skills they need in order to become happy, emotionally intelligent, and healthy adults.

Now, the foundation of good healthy discipline is respect, and the most common way that children lose respect and trust for their parents is harsh discipline that may humiliate the child like shouting and name-calling in a public setting. Healthy discipline is applied with mutual respect in mind, while still maintaining authority. It sometimes helps to remind yourself, and the child if you want, what the aim of any disciplinary action is. You want to discipline your child to (Canadian Paediatric Society, 2004):

- Promote emotional intelligence.

- Protect the child from danger.

- Help the child learn self-discipline.

- Help the child develop a healthy conscience.

- Help the child develop a healthy sense of responsibility and accountability.

- Help your child understand right from wrong

- Help your child understand their values.

The "do as I say and not as I do" approach to discipline can also result in a loss of respect from child to parent because this inconsistency causes confusion in the mind of the child. As the child grows, they may start to believe that it is alright to say and mean different things which may lead to the development of certain negative characteristic traits such as lying. In addition, saying and meaning two different things makes it difficult to understand who you are as a person and may make the child feel lost and confused in later life.

Consequences

Help your child understand that every action has a reaction, and negative actions have negative reactions. When your parents' senses are tingling, and you have a feeling that your daughter is about to start arguing about not letting her stay out with her friends until the early hours of the morning, take some time and remind her that all actions have reactions. Explain your train of thought and your reason behind your decision. If she goes ahead and starts the argument anyway and says she's staying out all night regardless of what you say, then it's time to lay out some consequences. It's important to always follow through with the consequences and not back down. Remember, this is going to benefit your child in the long run.

If your four-year-old doesn't want to clean up after herself after explaining to her why you want her to, then again, it's time to lay out some consequences. If the consequence is that she won't be allowed to play with any other toys until all the LEGO blocks are in the box, you need to follow through. It might be difficult, but don't give in to that sweet smile and sparkly eyes.

Don't Respond

If your child isn't in immediate danger and you know that you have given them plenty of attention, sometimes it's a good idea to let nature take its course. That way your child will understand that consequences are real reactions to their actions and not just things that you made up to make sure they behave. If your toddler doesn't want to pick up their toys, let it slide. Later, when she's looking for her favorite stuffed animal before going to bed, she's going to have a hard time finding him in that mess. Once the situation has played out, make it a learning experience, and explain that this was the reason you wanted her to clean up in the first place. I doubt she'll argue next time you ask her to put her toys away.

Chores

A great way to teach older children discipline is to allocate chores to do around the house. This teaches them responsibility and self-reliance and also equips them with skills that they will one day need when they have their own houses. Good and bad behavior can be addressed by decreasing or increasing chores. Remember, chores are different from the harsh punishment of intense manual labor. Punishing a child by making him paint the whole house is different from allocating chores daily or weekly.

Taking Away Privileges

When taking away a privilege in response to bad behavior, it's important not to cave and let your child off the hook earlier than agreed on. You know how the doctor says that you have to finish the whole course of antibiotics when you have some sort of infection, even if you feel better after just two days? Well, it's the same with punishment. You need to follow through with the specified period of punishment, even if the child seems a little better behaved after a week or so. Reminding your child that privileges are not needed is also a good way to instill a sense of gratitude.

When It's Done, It's Done

Don't harp on past experiences of bad behavior in a negative light. If you want to refer to the situation, always refer to it in a positive light and include how you can see that your child has grown from that experience.

Healthy Discipline Through the Developmental Years

Birth to 12 months

Discipline and routine around this time in your child's development is usually around feeding, sleeping, and playing. Allocating specific times to sleep and play as well as scheduling feeding at the same time each day helps regulate the child's autonomic functioning and provides a sense of predictability and safety (Canadian Paediatric Society, 2004). Babies learn by watching what you do and mimicking your actions, so set examples of behaviors by acting them out yourself. Use positive language and associate words with actions or objects.

One to Three Years of Age

At this age, discipline is usually aimed at safety and the prevention of destructive behavior. Continue to associate actions and objects with words. For example, if your child is reaching for your cup of tea, you can move the tea away and firmly say, "No, hot." Redirecting a child's focus from dangerous activities, like playing with a glass cup, to safer activities, like playing with a soft toy, is relatively easy.

Between the ages of two and three, temper tantrums will begin as your child will become frustrated at their limitations. At this point, your child is starting to recognize what's allowed and what isn't and may even start to test the boundaries. As your child begins to master their new skills and situations, tantrums will become more common, and it's important to balance these high-energy moments with naps (Sege & Siegel, 2018).

At this stage, it's important to start to manage aggressive behavior and practicing calming techniques on your child. Talking calmly to a child at this stage has been shown to soothe them and help them calm down. In addition, bribing children with activities or treats that make them happy and forget about their irritation, although not always ideal, can be a great way to help your child maneuver through their feelings. While your child is calm or happy in the middle of eating their ice cream sundae or as you push them on the swings at the playground, talk to them calmly about their outburst, and let them know that what they did was wrong.

Three to Five Years of Age

At this stage, your child is still trying to understand the world around them. They are only starting to realize that their actions have reactions and will no doubt continue to test the limits. This is the perfect age to begin assigning chores like putting toys away after using them or even helping you with things like tidying up. Give them little tasks like putting the pillows on the bed neatly or throwing a piece of paper away in the trash. When they accomplish these tasks, give them recognition and praise. This will keep them motivated.

Start introducing the idea of choice in simple things, like what to eat for dinner or which swing they want to play on. Allow them to express their opinions—this way they learn things about themselves as well. At this stage in your child's development, it's important to allow them to be vocal about their feelings and prompt them with questions when you can see that they are unable to express themselves completely. Dealing with attitude and aggression at this stage can be particularly difficult, but since your child is now aware of themselves, communication can begin.

Six to 12 Years of Age

Independence starts to grow at this stage, and your child should have a firm idea of right and wrong. Steadfast rules should be set at this stage about expected behavior, and disciplinary measures should be put in place. By this stage, the child should be given more responsibility in their household chores and allowed to make some decisions in the home environment, like whether to go to the beach or the park this Saturday. Once again, your child's opinions, likes, and dislikes are important and valid, so treat them as such.

Since they are now a school-going age, talk about the possible choices and situations they may be put in as well as the consequences of choices. Also, talk about family expectations, and provide a balance of privileges and responsibilities (American Academy of Pediatrics, 2019).

Adolescents and Teens

At this point, your child craves a sense of autonomy and is now independent and has developed their decision-making skills. It's important to lay some ground rules, and enforce the idea of action and consequence while still offering love and support. The chores that they are allocated will become more involved, and their interests will be continuously changing. It's important at this stage to also talk about the possible choices that they will be faced with, and praise the choices to avoid harmful substances such as drugs and other behaviors you think your child should avoid. At the same time, be open to your child's opinions and beliefs, and ensure that they understand their values and where they stand in the family setting.

Chapter 10:

Parenting Styles

Regardless of the parenting style you choose to practice, connecting with your child is the most important part of parenting, and some say that it's the reason your child is able to be parented. Think about it: Wouldn't you rather learn about life from someone close to you than learning about the difference between right and wrong from the mailman you see daily but don't really have a connection with? Don't be the mailman in your child's life.

Building a relationship with your child will give them a sense of security, but it is also important for all areas of child development. Studies have shown that poor parent-child relationships during the developmental years have not only negatively affected all relationships of the child during their adult years but also decreased the sense of the child's self-worth and self-esteem, ultimately leading to a low quality of life in adulthood (McAdams et al., 2016).

It's important to maintain your chosen style of parenting while connecting with your child to ensure that healthy boundaries are still set, and there is consistency in your parenting technique. If you are a no-nonsense kind of parent who is strict about adhering to the household rules, you cannot flip the switch and become a fun parent who no longer believes in rules to build a closer relationship with your child. This change in behavior and inconsistency in your parenting technique will teach your child that it's okay to change who you are for others, which is not something that you want your child to cling to. In addition, this approach usually results in a loss of respect for the parent on the part of the child. Don't forget: You are a parent before you are a friend. While I endorse the idea of boundaries and remembering your role in your child's life, I believe that the ways in which you can connect with your child work with all parenting techniques.

Before we get into how to better connect with your child and nurture meaningful relationships, let's quickly go through the different parenting techniques that exist. Remember, there is no right and wrong technique, and usually the choice of type of parenting is based on how we, ourselves, were parented. That's how we create our instruction manuals, remember? There are various studies that have been done on the many parenting styles and techniques, and although some show more favorable outcomes than the others, the ultimate deciding factor is the quality of life of the child as they grow into adulthood.

Take some time to read through these styles and try to identify one or two that relates most to the way you parent your child or children.

Authoritative Parenting

This is not to be confused with the authoritarian style of parenting. Authoritative parents are strict but still warm and comforting. This style of parenting is one of the best and allows a healthy parent-child relationship while still instilling a sense of discipline and clearly defining roles within the family hierarchy. There are boundaries and rules and the parent is clearly defined as the authoritative figure. Children are still encouraged to share their views and opinions, and there is open communication without fear of punishment; however, there are still high expectations of the child which leads to the development of their sense of accountability for their actions. Children who are raised in this manner show high levels of emotional intelligence and are extremely resilient. They are comforted by the fact that they know that their parents are there for them and understand the importance of discipline.

An example of this type of parenting would be if your child comes home with a low mark on their exam. As the parent, you sit down and review the paper with your child. You positively comment on the things that your child got right and motivate them to work harder on the things they got wrong. You reinforce the fact that you are always there to help if they are struggling with anything (Jarvis & Roffe, 2020, p. 63).

Although this type of parenting is often thought of in a negative light, it is usually not as disciplinarian as it may seem. In the above example, you might take away a certain privilege because your child did not do as well as they could have, but you would explain why you were taking away the privilege and would teach the child the importance of setting and achieving goals that are attainable. If you know that your child is not particularly good at math, for example, you should obviously encourage your child to work on it and not just believe that they will never be good at it. This is when your authority comes in. It's not necessarily that you want your child to become a mathlete—you just want to teach them that they can achieve anything that they put their mind to. Your kid could end up being the next Michelangelo and may never end up using calculus or trigonometry in their lives, but they will always remember that time they conquered it!

Attachment Parenting

This style of parenting involves a sort of obsession with the child—that is usually to ensure safety and comfort. The parent becomes attached to the child and is usually present for all major experiences as they grow. This could mean going to your child's first concert with them, shadowing them on their first date, and even volunteering to be the chaperone at all school outings and excursions. Although this type of parenting seems obsessive, studies have actually shown that children who grow up in this type of environment feel supported and have a higher sense of self-worth. They have shown to be emotionally intelligent, since they are able to express themselves openly without judgment and are more supportive and comforting because they have experienced this while growing up (Jarvis & Roffe, 2020, p. 65).

On the other hand, children might sometimes feel a bit smothered and think their parents are overprotective, especially as they grow into their teenage years. It's important to put yourself in your child's shoes sometimes. Think about when you were their age: Did you want your father sitting a table away on your first date? Remember, it's healthy for you not to know every single detail about your child's life as they grow. More than that, it makes it worthwhile when they volunteer information to you. It will make you feel happy that they trust you and want to share personal parts of themselves with you.

An example of this type of parenting is taking a whole week off work, even though you don't have much leave left, since your child is going away on a camping trip with school, so you have volunteered to go along with them and be the chaperone.

Helicopter Parenting

In this type of parenting, there's usually less immediate contact and involvement in the child's life—it can come in many different forms. Parents hover over their child in order to protect them from the surrounding world. Often, parents act on behalf of their child in this style of parenting. Since they don't want to seem too involved in their child's life, they try not to embarrass their child by being too forward in their attempts to keep them safe. For example, if a child is failing at a subject in school, the parent will set up a meeting with the teacher, without letting the child know, to discuss their performance and what could be causing their drop in grades. On the other side of the spectrum, helicopter parenting might leave parents looking over the child's shoulder as they do their homework or enrolling them in activities without their input (Higuera, 2019).

This type of parenting allows parents to identify any problems or issues during the early stages of a child's development, for example, if they're being bullied but are too shy to talk about it. The involvement of the parents in the child's life, while still giving the child a sense of autonomy—though somewhat false—offers the child support. Parents who practice this style of parenting may, however, come across as controlling and become slightly obsessive. This type of parenting can easily progress to a more intense form of attachment parenting. This could lead to an invasion of privacy on the part of the child and makes it harder for parents to let go of their children and live their own lives as they grow.

Uninvolved Parenting

Uninvolved parenting, sometimes known as neglectful parenting, has more unfavorable overtones. It is a style of parenting in which parents do not attend to their children's wants and desires beyond the fundamentals of food, clothes, and shelter. Parents provide minimal supervision, discipline, or care to these children. All too frequently, children are left to grow alone and live independently.

This type of parenting is often referred to as neglectful. The parent usually chooses not to get involved in their child's life or is unable to do so for some reason. Although this type of parenting leads to strong, self-reliant, and confident children, the lack of involvement hinders emotional development and could have a negative impact on the child's relationships. Not many children who are raised this way live a life of good quality, and they often develop mental health issues such as depression, anxiety, and attachment issues to partners and friends. It leads to a confused state of mind. Parents often provide little or no supervision and show little warmth and affection toward their children (Cherry, 2019).

There could be many reasons for parents behaving this way. Parents who have an uninvolved parenting style are usually raised by parents who are uninvolved and dismissive. They repeat the same behaviors when they become adults. Other parents who exhibit this style may simply be too preoccupied with their own life to take a practical learning approach to dealing with their children. In some situations, parents may be so busy with their own issues (being stressed, going through a hard time, or battling substance misuse) that they overlook how detached they are with their kids or are incapable of providing the comfort and support their kids need.

Authoritarian Parenting

The strictest in the land! This style of parenting involves setting extremely high standards and expectations. Parents who usually practice this style believe in reward and punishment and show little affection toward their children. Don't misunderstand me: Authoritarian parents love their children very much—they just believe that open affection does not raise successful children. They want the best for their children, just like all parents do. In this type of parenting, there are strict rules that are laid out, and going against these rules can result in serious consequences. Jeff Nalin, an award-winning licensed clinical psychologist, says,

> . . . children whose behavior is largely dependent on a strict regimen of dos and don'ts will base their own self-worth on whether or not they have obeyed the rules put into place by their parents. As well, this emphasis on cause and consequence hinders a child's natural ability to make choices—choices that may have a direct impact on his or her self-esteem. (Perry, 2019)

Although this type of parenting raises well-behaved individuals who are dedicated and have exceptionally high levels of self-discipline, they also rank low on self-esteem and have relatively lower levels of happiness in their adult lives. Children raised this way also find it difficult to have meaningful relationships and prefer independence or "alone time" (Jarvis & Roffe, 2020, p. 73) This parenting style has a low level of parent involvement and a high level of parental expectation. Authoritarian parents are cold and distant, and they are tough with their kids if they fail to achieve their expectations. For them, to regulate desirable action, rules should always be utilized.

Free-Range Parenting

Although many experts are quite conflicted about the idea of "free-range parenting," there are certain positive outcomes to this style. It's important to note that this type of parenting is not a careless or uninterested style but rather endorses the idea that children should enjoy some carefree time to themselves.

It works on the idea that both parents and children deserve some time apart from each other to also self-reflect and have experiences independent of the other. As long as the child is not in immediate danger, allowing them to engage themselves in their environment can help build self-confidence. While the notion of free-range parenting differs from family to family, it fundamentally involves giving your children responsibility at an early age. These tasks differ depending on the child's skills. For instance, examples could be going to the park alone, riding a bicycle to school, or taking the subway without assistance.

This type of parenting raises creative and innovative children that are self-reliant and have a good self-esteem. They are also more independent and have better relationships, as well as a greater sense of emotional intelligence (Morin, 2020). It's crucial to understand that free-range parenting isn't the same as detachment because mother and father are still extremely involved. They'll teach important life lessons to their children, support them through hardships, and educate them about safety measures. When it comes to putting these teachings into practice in real life, however, free-range parents step back and allow their children to take the lead. They expect a greater sense of independence, courage, problem-solving skills, creativity, and more from their children.

Permissive Parenting

This is the exact opposite of authoritative parenting, with no stringent rules, no punishment, and almost no consequences for the child's actions. It's all about building a stronger bond with your child with the intention of being their friend and equal. The child, in this case, has complete freedom to make their own decisions.

Although the biggest positive outcome of this type of parenting is the parent-child bond that develops, there are obvious fallbacks when it comes to being your child's "equal." Children brought up in these kinds of households usually have trouble with authority, having not been exposed to the concept regularly enough (Morin, 2019b).

There is little evidence to show that one parenting style is superior to the other, and in all reality, there is a time and place for all the different styles of parenting.

You might be a permissive parent for some of the time while still being authoritative and setting clear goals. You might clearly define boundaries and your authority while still sharing moments with your child where you feel like best friends. You might even practice an authoritarian approach when it comes to things like academics or goal-setting methods, but be more permissive when it comes to things like their social interactions and how late they can stay up.

Parents don't always fall into one of these categories, so don't get discouraged if you're permissive at times and authoritarian at others. However, research shows that authoritative parenting is the most effective parenting style. However, even if you relate with other parenting styles, you can take measures to be a more authoritative parent. You can keep a pleasant relationship with your child even while maintaining your influence in a healthy manner if you are dedicated and committed to being the best parent. The most important thing when parenting is raising happy, healthy, and emotionally intelligent individuals that will be able to find their way with the skills that you have equipped them with (Morin, 2019).

Chapter 11:

Connecting With Your Child

In the long run, although we all want to be best friends with our children, it might be better to maintain the authority of a parent. Don't get me wrong: Being friends with your children is not necessarily a bad thing. In fact, it's shown to build trust and a deeper relationship than that of parents who don't make an effort to become friends with their kids, but like I said in the previous chapter, there's a time and place for everything.

Listen

When your child is having a tantrum or your teenager is whining about their awful day at school, put your phone away, close the laptop, make a cup of tea, sit with them, and listen. More importantly, listen attentively.

When your toddler has lost their mind because they realized that they can never be a giraffe—trust me, I've heard it all)—calmly explain that the best way to deal with this is to talk it out. Think of their favorite treat and say something like, "Let's talk about this over a cup of tea and some ice cream, sweetheart," you have naturally drawn their attention to a more attractive use of their time, and once you have your cup of tea and they have their ice cream, as you sit at the table, let them talk about their feelings and what made them so angry or concerned before. Create a sort of tradition that will positively impact your family. Before you know it, your teenager will be making your cup of tea and sitting you down, ready to share the details of their horrible day with you. This sort of tradition will bring your child a sense of security and reinforce the fact that you will always listen to them, no judgment—just care and support.

A friend of mine dropped by one evening for a cup of tea to get a break from the hustle and bustle of mommy life. She was feeling a little overwhelmed because her toddler's tantrums had become difficult to manage. She said that they would just be driving and her daughter would suddenly insist on listening to a different song on the radio. If she didn't change the song fast enough, her daughter would start to scream and cry. Then, when it was time to get ready to go to school in the morning, her daughter would run around and insist on playing with her toys which would make her late for work. If she started to clean up the toys and firmly tell her daughter to get ready, she would kick up a fuss and plop herself on the couch while crying her eyes out. My friend looked exhausted, and I remember her commenting that motherhood was not what they made it out to be in the movies. It seemed evident to me that my friend thought that a mother-daughter relationship would exist from the start, and she wouldn't need to put in any effort to develop one—she was wrong. I told her to take some time and actually talk to her daughter, even when she's screaming or crying. Instead of screaming back at her, I told her to make herself a cup of tea, make her daughter a cup of hot chocolate, sit at the kitchen table, and really listen to what her daughter had to say. It turns out, there was a kid at school who was troubling her. She didn't know how to deal with the feelings that were building up inside her, and she didn't know how to express herself. That's why she hated going to preschool, and she would kick up a fuss when it was time to get ready or on the car ride there. The kid had stolen her crayons and had even pulled her hair. After that, I remember my friend being closer than ever to her little girl, who's now 17 years old and talks to her mom about almost everything.

Bedtime Catch-up Sessions

At the end of the day, when your child is ready to go to bed, sit with them and snuggle a little bit. Talk to them about anything at all. Children are curious creatures, and when they are little, topics of conversation are never really exhaustive. As your child grows, you can stand at their door and knock to show that you respect their space and their autonomy, then ask if they have some time for a quick bedtime catch-up session.

A distant cousin of mine is having his first child soon. His wife is almost due, so we gathered for a family dinner about a month ago. We all reminisced about our childhoods and how we wish we were children again without the headaches of mortgages and debt. My cousin reflected and told us about how his favorite part of the day was always bedtime because his father used to sit on his bed next to him, and they would just talk about their days. He knew every one of his father's co-workers and all their troubles. He knew the life stories of all his father's friends. He knew when his father was struggling with something at work. He knew all about his father's side of the family and what they were doing with their lives. He knew what his father always wanted to be when he grew up (a gardener) and his favorite plants and flowers. He told us how privileged he felt to be a part of every aspect of his father's life, even if it was just in the stories he heard. As he grew, he began sharing his own stories with his father at bedtime, and when his mother passed away when he was only 12 years old, when his father did not have the energy to sit on his bed and talk about his day, he would sit on his father's bed instead and talk about his own day. They were each other's support, and my cousin wished only the same hope for his unborn child: that he will be able to feel the love and support that he himself had felt from his own father.

Take Them Along on Your Errands

As I mentioned in an earlier chapter, the number one reason that children act out is their need for attention when they are not getting enough. Taking your toddler with you to run a couple of errands like picking up the dry cleaning or grocery shopping is a great way to give them the one-on-one attention they need and allows you to spend quality time with them. Quality one-on-one time with children is very important, as it allows them to feel loved and also builds the bond between parent and child. This is especially important in a large family of many children. You might notice one child being particularly irritable or angry lately, and this might be because in the hustle and bustle of everyday life, you haven't taken a moment to spend some quality time with them. This is also a great opportunity to talk about emotions and feelings, and develop your child's emotional intelligence. While riding in the car, you can chat about anything and everything, and you can use the opportunity to find out what your child is interested in at this stage in their lives.

One of my neighbors had been struggling with their teenage son recently. The kid just didn't want to communicate or spend any time at all with his parents. He would spend his time at his friend's place after school, and on the weekends, he would take small jobs here and there to earn a little extra cash. My neighbors felt like they were losing their son, and you could see that it was taking a toll on them. They seemed unhappy and stressed out. At family dinners, the kid would eat his food quietly and respond with one-word answers. I suggested that they take him with them shopping one day. They needed some supplies for a camping trip that the boy's father was planning with his friends. While walking through the shopping complex, the boy's mother noticed that he stopped for a moment outside a music shop, so she decided to take him in. They walked around the shop, and the kid seemed to be drawn to the drum set at the back. After a little prompting, my neighbor found out that her son had recently taken an interest in music and was spending his time after school at his friend's house who was teaching him how to play the drums. The job he had taken on the weekends was to save up for a drum set that he found on eBay, and he really wanted to pursue a career in music. At this point, my neighbor had felt closer to her son than she had in years.

Invite Your Child Into Your Daily Routine

During the early years of childhood, your child is still developing their skills and interests. Allowing them to engage in activities like cooking with you is a great way for them to begin to explore their likes and their dislikes. In addition, it will allow you to spend quality time with them which will improve your bond and relationship. Your presence will always be remembered when your child thinks back to their first cooking experience or the first time they planted a seed in the garden.

Different activities will also stimulate different parts of your child's brain and help build new neural connections. In addition, activities like mixing cake batter or measuring a teaspoon of baking powder can fine-tune your child's motor skills.

Believe it or not, cooking or baking can significantly aid in the cognitive development of your child. Word and feeling association are a great way to develop your toddler's cognitive abilities. When cooking, baking, or engaging in any activity at all, ask your toddler to hold something in their hands and describe how it feels. When they struggle to describe the feeling, suggest words that they can add to their vocabulary. Counting and the idea of numbers can be introduced in the measurements that you use while cooking. Allow your child to taste the food and describe how it is (AdventHealth, 2019).

Check In About the Plan for the Day

At breakfast, check in with your child about what they have planned for the day. This way, you will have an idea of what their day looks like, and soon, it will become a habit for them to tell you what the plans are. Ask your toddler what it is they are most excited about, or ask your teenager what they think their favorite teacher has planned for the day. You can follow up on the plan at the end of the day by asking your child how their day was. Another important thing to remember is that although these things are laid out in this chapter like a sort of to-do list, in everyday life, these things should come naturally. Don't force it or overthink it—let it flow naturally. You shouldn't be keeping a check list of all the things you have to do to connect with your child. Trust me when I say, the natural love and care that comes with being a parent will have you naturally asking your child to help you cook or organically engaging in serious conversation on the car ride home from school (Wright, 2019).

A friend of my husband's was complaining about not knowing anything about his eight-year old child's life. The kid was quiet and reserved, nothing at all like his parents, and they seemed to be having trouble with communication. He said that his wife was losing her mind trying to get through to him. I told him to start small, and just sit down at the breakfast table and ask about what they had planned for the day; then, at the end of the day, ask if he did everything he planned. Don't force the conversation or pry too much—that'll make them feel a little threatened. After a week or so of breakfast conversation, the two of them were inseparable. Later, after the boy was having a little trouble at school, he was diagnosed with an autism spectrum disorder, and the therapist was intrigued by the relationship the child had built with his father, despite his social awkwardness and inability to effectively communicate.

Share Parts of Yourself With Them

As a parent, you can't always be expecting to know absolutely everything about your child while sharing little with them. Tell them stories about when you were growing up and things that you have always wanted to do. Tell your toddler about how much you loved coloring when you were their age and how you were obsessed with your favorite stuffed animal. Tell your teenager about your first crush and how you and your partner met. Tell your adolescent daughter about your first heartbreak and how happy you are that it didn't work because it led you to your partner. Sharing is a two-way street, and it will make your child feel closer to you in more ways than one.

An acquaintance of mine would complain nonstop about their 15-year-old daughter and how she was always pushing the boundaries and acting out. It was clear that the woman preferred a harsh type of parenting and was a no-nonsense kind of person, which I respected. I asked her how much of herself she shared with her daughter, and she said that she was the parent and didn't need to share anything with her daughter. After I explained that all relationships in life, including a parent-child relationship, is a two-way street, she decided to take my advice into consideration. About five months later, I met her while grocery shopping and she seemed happier and more relaxed. She told me that her relationship with her daughter was better than ever after she began sharing her own stories as well.

Get the Photo Album!

During your child's teenage years, or when they're old enough to appreciate it, take a trip down memory lane with them. You can get your old albums from when you were growing up, and tell them stories about your childhood. You can also get their albums from when they were growing up, and tell them stories about times that they probably don't have memory of.

Tell Stories

Sit your child in your lap or sit close to them on the couch, snuggle up, and tell them a story. It can be a story about anything at all. As a father, you might want to tell your little daughter a story about how you stood up to your boss at work. You can call yourself a king and your boss a giant ogre who was out to hurt all those in the land; tell her how the king eventually captured the ogre.

Steal a Hug Whenever You Can

At any moment of the day, simply embrace your child, and shower them with love and affection (Hallet, 2020). Hugs increase trust, reduce anxiety, and deepen bonds. Plus, the benefits are reciprocated. Physical affection, both giving and receiving, is beneficial to both you and your child. You develop a special link with your child the moment you hold them for the first time, and this bond must be nourished throughout infancy. Your attachment will change as your child grows, but the urge to feel your loving touch will never go away. Many adults are concerned that embracing a sulking child may reinforce negative behavior. This, however, is a myth. When a child has an emotional tantrum, they're expressing their feelings in response to something in their surroundings. They aren't being obstinate or attempting to ruin the day of others. Hugging your child during these severe emotional temper tantrums will help them stay calm, show them that you are there to comfort them through difficult times, and prevent an emotional breakdown.

Spend Time Outside

Spending time together outside, either by playing a game or just walking around, is a great way to spend some time together. Engaging in fun activities with your child on a daily basis, especially if your child is in control of the games, can make them feel a lot calmer and less anxious, as well as confident, strong, and obedient. Sibling rivalry is also considerably reduced when parents spend meaningful time with each child. Planning activities such as a walk in the park, a family road trip, a visit to a neighboring green area, or even a backyard match can help you bond with your child. These small daily doses of outdoor time prove to be extremely beneficial in a child's health and well-being, and they make longer weekend getaways or family holidays feel less strange and more enjoyable for everybody.

Listen to Music Together

Music allows children of all ages to express themselves. Even infants respond to music by swaying, bouncing, or moving their hands. Many toddlers make up tunes and sing to themselves while playing, with little self-consciousness. Schoolchildren try singing in groups and potentially learn to play an instrument. Introduce your toddlers to your favorite songs and genres of music. You can have sing-alongs in the car and even dance parties on Saturday nights. Ask your teenager to introduce you to some of their favorites and give it a chance. Play a mix of your songs and theirs in your car rides and on road trips. That way, subconsciously, the whole family will know the lyrics to each other's favorite songs, which makes for a nice singing session. Children look back on memories like these fondly because memories are associated with feelings.

Become Your Child's Pen Pal

A great way to teach your child linguistic and communication skills while still building a strong bond and connection with them is to write letters to each other. Pick a day in the week where you should both expect a letter from the other. That way, you can write your letter any day in the week but only deliver it on the decided day. Your letters can be about anything at all. As a parent, you might want to give them some advice and remind them how much you love them. Your child might write to you about their day, how they are feeling, or even about their new crush at school, depending on how close you are. You can keep these letters, and so can your child, to remind you of these times.

Try New Things Together

As your child grows and enters their adventurous years, make a joint list of things you want to do, like hike the nearby waterfall trail or try sushi. Then, take the time to actually follow through with it!

I know of a father-son duo who have climbed almost every great mountain peak in the Northern Hemisphere. The father is a plastic surgeon, and the son is a lawyer in California. They found an activity that they enjoyed doing together, and they ran with it. The father has two other sons, one he takes long fishing trips with, and the other he flips houses with. He has built a different bond with all three of his children by finding what each of them loved and doing it with them.

Chapter 12:

The Art of Mindfulness

Even though mindfulness is not a defined skill domain within emotional intelligence, practicing mindfulness may help children enhance various aspects of their emotional intelligence, like emotional self-discovery, stress tolerance, and impulsive behavior. Since being more aware is at the heart of mindfulness, it combines a vital component with emotional intelligence: self-awareness. Remember that the aim of this chapter is to give you a brief outline of mindfulness and to summarize how it can be another tool you can use to help your child develop emotional intelligence abilities.

Mindfulness implies focusing your thoughts on yourself or the environment in the current moment. One of the most fundamental aspects of mindfulness is not criticizing yourself or your ideas. In fact, the goal is to stay so concentrated on whatever you're doing right now that worries about the future or recollections from the past fade away. When mindfulness is properly practiced, it allows a person to relax by remaining physically and mentally attentive in the current moment. The purpose of mindfulness meditation is to become more relaxed, and it generally involves deep breathing or muscle relaxation.

Mindfulness and Emotional Intelligence: What Is the Connection?

Simply put, emotional intelligence aims to help people be more conscious of their feelings and why they experience them, as well as to successfully channel those emotions to regulate themselves, their actions, and their interactions. When mindfulness is properly exercised, it can help a person become more aware and relaxed. Mindfulness can help children develop emotional intelligence abilities, such as empathy, self-awareness, and emotional regulation, if it is practiced correctly. Children nowadays are under more stress than ever before, whether it's due to competition to be at the top, parental divorce, financial difficulty, or parents who are preoccupied with work or the health of one of their children.

As professional sport possibilities for children start at the age of four, childhood strain has risen considerably in the last 50 years. With countless events to choose from, many parents find themselves rushing from one activity to the next with kids who may or may not be enthusiastic about the activity. Since it includes another pressure on the body, the hectic pace of the schedule causes stress in both adults and children. Mindfulness can aid in the slowing down of events and the restoration of calm.

Difference Between Mindfulness and Meditation

There are many different types of meditation, and one of them is mindfulness. One of the most popular forms of meditation, this includes sitting down and reciting a mantra or chanting a profound phrase just to yourself or out loud. The idea is to immerse yourself in the present moment and create a mental "blank slate." Mindfulness, on the other hand, promotes active awareness of one's surroundings, physiological sensations, feelings, and ideas. The purpose of mindfulness is to maintain a current concentration, letting go of the future and past in order to focus solely on the here and now. Sitting, walking, or lying down can all be used to cultivate mindfulness.

Although mindfulness can lead to relaxation, it is not the primary purpose of mindfulness. Rather, the goal is to remain in the present moment and increase awareness. The majority of the research into the advantages of mindfulness has been conducted on adults. Clinicians have created programs that use mindfulness practices to help people manage chronic pain and relieve stress. Furthermore, mindfulness practices have been utilized to treat depression, anxiety, eating disorders, borderline personality disorder, and addictions (Kanoy, 2013).

Ways to Practice Mindfulness

Observing, articulating, and engaging are all skills that are required for mindfulness. It can be centered around an object, the surroundings, a body sensation, emotions, or feelings, with the level of difficulty increasing as the child progresses to a more interior focus on thinking. Nonjudgmental participation is an important feature of mindfulness. Keeping those criteria in mind, start with an item or something from the surroundings for the child to focus on.

Observe What's in Front

Consider your child's personality and what would work best for him. Children who are more passive may find it beneficial to practice mindfulness by sitting still. Put an item in front of the child, and ask them to look at it and describe it out loud or in a notebook. A more energetic youngster could like a mindfulness walk through a garden or several views of a blooming flower, a car, or your home.

Observing What's Around

Select an activity that appeals to your child's interests or disposition once again. A child who is interested in astronomy could use a telescope or sit around with a parent to observe them. You may take your child on a stroll in a park or even to the zoo, and let them observe to study their behavior. The objectives are to free the mind of what will happen tomorrow or what happened yesterday and to notice and explain what is happening right now. Children should practice being nonjudgmental so that when it comes to describing themselves, they will be able to do so without being judged. To put it another way, rather than stating the monkeys are "nice," have them explain the actions they observe. Perhaps one of the monkeys reached the caged area's perimeter and approached you.

Observing Body Functions

A child engages in this sort of mindfulness exercise by paying close attention to his senses, usually focusing on body movement or feelings. It's possible to execute it in any position or while walking. Focusing on a single body part or experience, such as the feeling in the legs when walking or the sense of smell while walking through a park, is more helpful. The idea is to be entirely present in the moment and study his sensations before describing them. Children who've been practicing mindfulness can focus properly on their breathing sensations, which may take some time to perfect. The stomach area of your child's body will fall and rise as your child breathes in and out. When you're tense, your chest muscles take control of your breathing. Sit in a peaceful, comfortable spot with your child, each of you concentrating on long, calm breaths that cause the stomach area to rise and fall. What is it that your child notices? If you begin breathing properly, you may notice that the tips of your fingers get increasingly heated. Increased breathing dilates the blood arteries, allowing more blood to reach our extremities.

Observing Feelings

The most difficult kind of mindfulness to achieve is listening to your own feelings and emotions. It will, however, assist children in becoming conscious of their "self-talk." Do they have more negative or pleasant ideas and sentiments in their heads? Do you have negative thoughts first, then a negative feeling? Does the thought of a negative emotion occur first, accompanied by negative self-talk? There are numerous connections between mindfulness centered around thoughts, feelings, and mindfulness focused on actions. First and foremost, they both require your child to be conscious of their own self-talk. Second, they both assist someone in comprehending how unpleasant thoughts can lead to poor emotions. Finally, using mindfulness to question erroneous ideas through thoughts and feelings should improve your child's potential to increase positive self-talk, leading to less stress and improved self-esteem.

Emotional intelligence is a valuable talent to master in life. It can aid in the smoothing of relations and the foundation of natural feelings. When it comes to coping with your own and others' thoughts and feelings, each of these practices can take you to a new level of mastery. Mindfulness is a strong tool for separating an action from your reaction. These exercises help you improve EI by making you more aware of your own and others' emotions. It can also assist you in learning to properly apply and control your emotions through conscious action and thought.

Chapter 13:

What if It Gets Out of Hand?

Even if you try your best all the time trying to raise an emotionally intelligent child, there will be times when you will have no clue as to what to do. As children go about their days, trying to get along with everyone and deal with typical problems, it appears that their lives are full of possibilities, and the emotion training may not work then. Emotion training should not be viewed as a cure-all for unpleasant emotions. For one thing, it needs a certain amount of patience and inventiveness, so parents must be relatively undistracted (if not calm) in order to do it successfully. It also helps if the children are in a learning mood. You want to take advantage of opportunities when your child is most likely to be responsive. However, there are other instances where you could face certain unprecedented situations, which we will discuss below.

When You Are Short on Time

Parents today spend a lot of time together checking the time, attempting to get to childcare, school, and office on time. Although children's emotions are likely to emerge during these traumatic changes, these are not the best moments for a heart-to-heart talk. Emotion training is a process. We can't expect children to go through emotional experiences on a predetermined timetable; they aren't robots. In these situations, quick and effective action is necessary. In an ideal scenario, we'd always have time to sit down with our children and talk about their feelings as they arise. However, for the majority of parents, this is not always an option. As a result, it's vital to set aside time each day—preferably at the usual time each day—to communicate to your child without being rushed or interrupted. This is something that many families with small kids do before bedtime or during a bath. When you share duties with school-aged children and teenagers, such as cleaning dishes or hanging laundry, you can have heart-to-heart conversations. Drives to music classes or other trips on a regular basis provide extra opportunity. You can rest assured that topics will not be delayed forever due to time restrictions if you set up appropriate times for discussion.

When You Are Not in a Mood

When you're in a bad mood, it's tough not to vent your emotions on others around you. However, if your kids are the ones who bear the cost of your emotions, you may have severe repercussions. You will not only make them and yourself unhappy, but you can also become the parent you don't want to be. Empathizing with your child and listening to them needs a certain amount of creativity and energy. The capacity to think clearly and communicate properly can be hampered by extreme anger or tiredness. You may realize that you lack the ability and patience to sympathize and listen effectively. Furthermore, there may be instances when you are simply too exhausted to appropriately deal with your child's emotions. If this occurs, postpone the idea of "sit and talk" until you are able to acquire the rest or comfort you require to re-energize. This could be as simple as going for a walk, napping, taking a hot bath, or going to the movies.

You know that you are in a bad mood, and there's a high possibility your children will irritate you more: Work out a plan for how you'll react before that happens. Making a decision now, before you become furious, allows you to react accordingly. Make a list of possible reactions to what will most certainly happen, and take a look at it when you're upset. Following through on your predetermined plans will help you avoid taking your frustrations out on your children. If you feel that your ability to communicate with your child is being affected by weariness, anxiety, or anger, you may want to think about making some changes in lifestyle. A mental health counselor or other health care professional may be able to assist you in sorting through your options. You may try not to take your negative mood out on your children by learning to cope with unpleasant feelings, get appropriate help and make adjustments, and be frank with your children.

When There Are People Around

It's tough to develop connection and trust with your kids unless you spend some quality time alone with them. Emotion training best works when done one on one with your child rather than in front of other people such as family members, friends, or caregivers. This way, you won't embarrass your child. He will be able to answer you honestly without being concerned about what other people think of him. This suggestion is especially useful for families struggling with sibling rivalry issues. In the best-case scenario, an objective parent can act as a mediator while two or more siblings resolve their differences together. Emotion training, on the other hand, necessitates a higher level of empathy and attentiveness. It's difficult to openly empathize with two people who are at odds without having to pick sides. As a result, emotion training is more effective because neither the child nor the parent is concerned with a sibling's opinions, disruptions, or disagreements to what is being said. A child may be more likely to let down his guards and reveal true sentiments if given time alone with an empathetic adult.

Of course, the trick is to give each child equal treatment. Again, setting aside particular time for each kid on a regular basis can help to guarantee that this occurs. Parents should be conscious of how their own friends and senior relatives (notably grandparents) can affect their capability to empathize with and listen to their kids. When you take the advice of your own mother saying, "You need to be a little stricter with your child," it can be difficult to understand your children's feelings. If you're in a position that requires emotion training but you can't because of the involvement of others, keep in mind to do it later. You might want to tell your child (without humiliating him) that you're going to talk about it later. Remember to check up on them after that.

When You Have to Deal With Serious Misconduct

Bad behavior doesn't stop when your child grows out of diapers or even when they reach middle school. In fact, the teenage years can present some of the most difficult disciplinary issues for parents. Teens misbehave in a variety of ways, including crying, shouting, sulking, and rebelling. There's a valid reason for these bad behaviors. Teens are becoming more independent, but they still need the emotional stability to make well-informed decisions. The areas of the brain that handle decision making and impulsive behavior are still developing. Smoking, drinking, and engaging in sexual activity are just a few of the harmful teen habits that can result from a combination of immaturity and autonomy.

Therefore, you may need to exercise discipline that extends beyond the limit of simply setting some ground rules. You must express your dissatisfaction when your child does something that offends you and blatantly disregards your code of conduct. While you may understand the feelings that drive your child's misconduct, now is not the time to be sympathetic. Training your child emotionally to handle emotions which may have contributed to the misconduct can be delayed for now. Now is the opportunity to clearly express that you believe your child's behaviors were inappropriate and explain why.

Being strict on your child can be a little difficult especially when you are receptive to or feel responsible for your child's feelings and the reasons he may be behaving this way. Let's take an example. Suppose a couple about to get a divorce discovers that their teenage daughter has been skipping school, and they don't know how to react to that. In this situation, the parents may succumb to their daughter's emotions and sadness. They may be compelled to ignore the punishment and talk to their daughter about her feelings regarding the divorce. However, looking for reasons for the child's misconduct only harms her in the long term. The best way is to address her absence from school as one issue and her thoughts about the divorce as another.

When Your Child Is Being Manipulative

When a child manipulates, it may appear to be a devious and calculated trick. However, learning to manipulate is typically a natural process. Clinical psychologist, Dr. Susan Rutherford, writes about child manipulation in an article saying, "Children can learn how to get certain responses from their parents from a very young age. Typically not before 15 months, but some kids can understand this dynamic quickly" (Butler, 2020). When a child manipulates, it may appear to be a devious and calculated trick. Learning to manipulate, on the other hand, is typically a natural process. She talks about a small kid who wakes up wailing in the middle of the night. A parent rushes in to pick up the child and comfort him. The child quickly learns that this action will meet his requirements, and it becomes a habit. Every action has a goal and is a means to that goal. Our children act in certain ways because they desire or require certain things. Whether it's a stuffed toy, candy in the grocery aisle, or the skill to wheedle out of a task, many kids have figured out how to get around the process with little effort (Butler, 2020).

In such cases, if you as a parent decide to put a halt on giving your child emotional training, make sure you do it later. This is quite different from disapproving or dismissing parents who have an overarching parenting approach that involves ignoring emotion. They avoid powerful emotions totally because they are uncomfortable with them. Therefore, it's a wise decision to postpone your conversation to when it's more likely to be effective. If you say to your kid that you'll talk about something later, make sure you keep checking in on them. It's easier to see your child's manipulation as a means of getting his needs addressed instead of a cunning trick. When you address this behavior with interest instead of judgment, you might be able to figure out why he's acting this way. Parents are frequently ignorant of how their actions encourage the behaviors that lead to many teen-parent disputes. The concern that their child will be unhappy if they hear the word "no" or become upset with a choice that does not go in their favor is one such strategy that often plays with a parent's emotions. In reality, many parents are afraid that their child will have a breakdown and blame them for their sorrow.

When They Are Being Impulsive

As young children lack the cognitive and emotional abilities like adults, they seem impulsive naturally. When a baby becomes tired of being held, he doesn't wait for you to realize that his tantrums are an indication that he wants to be set down. Instead, he may simply cry loudly or tighten his body, making it impossible for you to embrace. A two-year-old who never misbehaves is something rare.

Impulse control is the skill to make decisions. If a child does anything inappropriate, it's easy to dismiss that as a "decision" if you act rashly because being impulsive is all about giving in to your emotions or sudden reactions. At its fundamental level, impulse control entails comprehending and managing emotions long enough to consider a choice before reacting. Impulses are never actually spontaneous—they appear to be so because they are carried out fast and without much thinking. Children can behave impulsively in a number of ways, including giving in to an urge to eat something or snatching a toy from another child, blabbering and copying others, cheating at a game, spending their whole weekly allowance at once, or hanging up the phone when angry. There are several possibilities to act impulsively. Every impulsive action involves a choice, but it isn't one that has been well considered. Well-considered decisions result in better outcomes.

There are four fundamental methods for teaching impulse control to children. To begin with, your child will be confronted with situations in which he will need to practice impulse control. You can prepare ahead of time to increase your chances of success. When he succeeds, congratulate him on his restraint by praising his acts of waiting or whatever else he achieved. Second, you may create a more appropriate atmosphere for impulse control, particularly if you believe your child is having difficulty learning this ability. Third, you can bring up impulse control when one of his friends or somebody else he knows exhibits the same. Discuss how the individual exercised control and the benefits that followed. Finally, you can use yourself as an example of impulse control.

Consistent disciplinary techniques are the most effective way to address child behavior issues. It's important to remember that it's common for children to regress from time to time. At the age of eight, your child may not respond to baby voices or become stubborn after months of cooperation. This is a common phenomenon, and it could simply be a part of your child's development. However, if your child's conduct isn't responsive to your discipline methods, or if their behavior is interfering with their schoolwork or peer interactions, consult your pediatrician. If there are any underlying developmental difficulties, learning challenges, or health conditions, they should be ruled out.

Chapter 14:

Setting Boundaries and Limits

While enjoying spending time with your children and building strong bonds and relationships is one of the best things you can do for their development, you need to guard yourself against what I like to call "slipping into the friendzone." You are, after all, your child's parent and not their friend. Slipping into the friend zone makes you more susceptible to manipulation by your child, and the truth is, sometimes you don't realize it until it's too late.

It's important to set boundaries and limits so that your authority is understood and accepted. Even when you are engaging with your child to connect with them, it's important that they understand you love them and care for them, probably more than anybody in the world ever will, and you want the best for them. However, you are also their parent, and there must always be that sense of respect from their side. Like I said before, I've seen all kinds of parents, and some prefer the friend zone. However, being in the friend zone without boundaries and rules is simply a recipe for disaster. Once again, there is a time and place for everything.

The best way to describe parenting is as a kind of "mentorship." There are moments of learning, growth, and development, but there are also moments of friendship, fun, and happiness. There are moments of strict rules and discipline, but there are also moments where the rules go out the window or you make them up as you go along. As your child's mentor, your duty is to impart your knowledge based on your experiences unto them in the hope that they will positively grow and develop. Mentorship is the perfect balance between friend and disciplinarian.

Boundaries and limits, although important to establish a sense of discipline, also allows for a predictable routine that helps children feel safe and establish a comfortable sense of security. If boundaries and limits are not set, the balance of power in the household shifts toward the child, which is unbeneficial to both the parent and the child. Children who grow up in households where they hold too much power can grow up with a sense of entitlement and often have problems with figures of authority. There is a great difference between a good self-esteem and narcissism (Lee, 2021). These children seem to grow up with the belief that they know best and will find it difficult to learn from others' mistakes, leading them to make the same mistakes with the same consequences. Children who grow up this way begin to think that the world around them exists to serve them and find it difficult when entering the real world where people can be harsh, and they will not always get what they want. These children grow to be unequipped for life outside their household.

Boundaries and limits are like rules and consequences for not following the rules. By setting boundaries, children learn to modify their behavior to what's expected and accepted within the household setting, which will help them adapt as they grow as well (Lee, 2021).

Once again, when you are dealing with a toddler, it's important to remember that the brain of your child is not fully developed yet. This means that they are not equipped to be in charge of major decisions. When your child is between eight and 11 years of age, they begin to think more logically and seem to enjoy rules, predictability, and security. Then, after the age of 12, your child will begin to develop more abstract thinking and start to challenge your rules and push your limits. At this point, the prefrontal cortex of your child is still being fine-tuned, which means they're not fully in control of their impulsivity, decision making, and problem-solving skills yet. It is for these very reasons that during every stage of your child's development, you need to be in charge (Pozatek, 2015).

How to Set Boundaries

Establishing Calm, Respectful, and Effective Communication

Teaching children to express themselves in a respectful manner is a great way to maintain your sense of authority and also help your child develop the necessary communication skills that they will need in the future. The best way to do this is by yourself demonstrating how it's done. Remember, during the very early developmental stages in a child's life, most of their behavior is learned by watching you and mimicking what you do. As they grow, they continue to take cues from you and can often model their own behavior on yours. Speak to your child kindly and calmly but still firmly when you are disciplining them. Do not shout and try as hard as you can to remain collected and not lose your temper. Belittling children when they have done something wrong or when they express opinions that are different to you can decrease self-esteem and self-image among these individuals. In addition, children who are constantly shouted at or belittled grow to be adults with a poor sense of self-confidence which negatively affects their quality of life.

Having Rules

Create a set of household rules and display them in a communal area where they are clearly visible and can be referred to regularly, like on the fridge or on a wall in the main living area. Remember, the rules are not only for your child: They are for the entire family. Be absolutely clear about what will not be tolerated, and modify the rules as your child grows, making the modifications when your child has their first-time experiences of first-time encounters. For example, if your daughter is going on her very first outing with her friends, without any parents or adults, add a new rule to the list that says "When going out without parents, regular texts must be sent informing the parents 0f where you are at all times" or something similar. Of course, you might not phrase it as some sort of disciplinarian robot like I have.

Taming Tantrums

When you think "tantrum," the image of your wonderful child turning into some sort of monster usually comes to mind. Out of nowhere, your mostly well-behaved toddler turns into a screaming beast if you don't meet their demands, but children aren't the only ones who transform into something difficult to handle when a tantrum surfaces. Parents also transform from calm, loving, and caring figures into red-faced, human-sized loud speakers who yell and scream and then eventually give in to their child's demands. By that time, the parent usually feels defeated and questions whether they're failing at this parenting thing. Stop right there: Take a deep breath in, and calm yourself down.

Tantrums are a normal part of child development, which means that they're going to stick around for a little bit before leaving town for good. This means that you need to be able to manage them (Underwood, 2020). In fact, temper tantrums usually stick around from about one year of age until about four (Harrington, 2004). Once again, it's important to understand that the reason for temper tantrums is that your child's brain is not fully developed yet, which means that they lack physical, motor, and language skills, so they cannot truly express what they are feeling. Your child is unable to completely understand their emotions at this time as well, so the frustration of not being able to understand or express what they are feeling manifests as a temper tantrum.

First and foremost, when navigating through a tantrum, ensure that your child is safe. If your child is at risk of harming himself, others, or damaging anything in his/her general vicinity, move them somewhere safer. This usually applies if you are in a public setting and the tantrum is disruptive. Now, what I'm about to say next can be extremely difficult: Keep your cool and stay practical. Try not to become emotional, and remind yourself that this is a normal part of the developmental process. In extremely difficult situations, your child might be acting out physically, hitting or kicking you while screaming at the top of their lungs. It's important that you do not take this behavior personally, and try your best to diffuse the situation while still remaining logical in your actions.

In "A Field Guide to Taming Tantrums in Toddlers," published in *The New York Times* and written by Paul Underwood, he reports that Dr. Rebecca Schrag Hershberg, a clinical psychologist and renowned author, passed along an important piece of advice when he interviewed her. She said, "You as the parent are the thermostat, not the thermometer. Your goal is to reset the temperature, not take it and respond to it," (Underwood, 2020). If you are not calm, it makes it more difficult for your child to calm down. Take a deep breath and offer your child some positive and loving reassurance.

Next, the thing to do is try to identify what triggered the tantrum. Remember, tantrums are the only form of expression that your toddler might practice. This is because they don't know how to express themselves constructively yet. When your child is throwing a tantrum, they're really trying to communicate something to you that they don't have the skill to communicate effectively. Sometimes, the meaning behind a tantrum is simple and easy to identify, like if your child is tired or hungry. However, sometimes, it's deeper than that. If the trigger is less evident and the tantrum is in response to something like saying "no" to letting your toddler run with scissors or light a match, then it's time to become Sherlock Holmes and critically assess the situation.

Every tantrum is different, which means that there is no perfect rule that can apply to stop every type of tantrum for every child. There are, however, a series of different techniques that you can practice.

1. Affection

Offer to hug or hold your child to comfort them. Speak to them in a calming tone with love and care. This does not mean forcefully restraining your child or forcing them to hug you against their will—it's to comfort your child if they're feeling overwhelmed to let them know that you are here for them. While holding your child, talk about what they are feeling. You can ask specific questions like, "Are you feeling sad or angry?" Then, you can suggest solutions like, "I know you are sad that your dad isn't home from work yet, but he's going to be home in about an hour. What about if we play a game until he gets here?"

2. Distraction

If you are sure that the tantrum hasn't been triggered by anything serious, offer a distraction. For example, if your toddler is acting out because their sibling grabbed their toy or because the bird outside they grew attached to had suddenly flown away, offer another toy or take out the crayons and start drawing some birds with your child. Remember, as children grow, it will become more difficult to distract them because they will hold on tighter to their frustrations.

3. Ignore the Tantrum

Sit close to your child but refuse to engage in their behavior. Remember, you need to still be physically and emotionally available but focus on helping the child with something else. For example, if your child is screaming because her favorite T-shirt is in the wash and she can't wear it, ignore the screaming, and sit her down. Then, show her another T-shirt and talk about how much you like it.

Another technique is a sort of coping mechanism that you can teach your child as they are growing. It can be a breathing method or anything at all that can help your child center themselves and calm down.

You can teach your child to count down from 10 when they are feeling overwhelmed or even breathing in and out for ten breaths.

The most important thing is that once the tantrum is over, it's over. Resist the urge to punish the child or bring it up again. Once you have identified triggers, try to avoid them in general. If you have found that most of the tantrums are due to hunger or exhaustion, carry a snack with you when going out and plan your day so that you are home by nap time.

If your child's tantrums become particularly aggressive or excessive, it's important to see a professional for a full assessment.

Temper tantrums can often make you question your parenting skills, but remember it's a normal part of development; if you just keep your cool and navigate through it with love, care, and understanding, it'll be alright.

Chapter 15:

A Blissful Blended Family

Parenting in a blended family household can be particularly difficult and takes a bit of adjustment, for both the parent and child. Stepchildren who are over the age of 12 usually find it harder to adjust than younger children because they have already gone through their major developmental stages and are now aware of their emotions, their likes, and their dislikes. At these ages, children are going through their own changes with puberty and social interactions, and they find it difficult to adjust to a new home setup as well, which can often lead to a teenager lashing out or pushing boundaries. Although forming a new blended family can be challenging, it is often equally as rewarding.

Stepchildren often feel uncertain about the changes that accompany blending a family and how these new members of the family will now affect their relationship with their own parents. The adjustment from living with your family who you have grown up with and know to living with new stepsiblings who are basically strangers can be daunting. There is always the fear that stepsiblings will not get along or like each other.

When living in a blended family household, it's important as parents to have open-mindedness and not expect your new family to function in the same way that your previous one did. You cannot expect your stepchildren to behave in the same way that your children behave, simply because they have been brought up by different parents and have had different experiences than your own children. At first, the relationship between stepchild and stepparent might seem strained and difficult, but with open communication, patience, and mutual respect, it's very possible to develop a close bond and healthy relationship.

It usually takes between two and five years for a blended family to comfortably establish itself (Robinson, 2005). You have to remember, while you were dating your new partner, you were a playmate and a fun guest to have over during the holidays. Now that you are an authoritative figure in the household, your stepchildren might find it more difficult to adjust to your discipline. The amusing and quirky habits that your partner's teenage stepdaughter exhibited may lose their charm once you are living under the same roof. In the same way, while she once saw you as a friend and confidant, the change in roles might be difficult for her to accept.

The parent-child relationships are not the only thing that becomes challenging when settling into a blended family household. The relationship between you and your new partner will also change, especially when it comes to the way each of you practice parenting. When you are dating and in the love bubble, these are things that rarely come to mind, but when you are an authoritative parent, and you find out that your partner is a helicopter parent, there's bound to be disagreements. This, in turn, has a great impact on the children in the household as well. You see, children need parental consistency in order to develop into functional adults. Otherwise, they become confused and begin to test the boundaries. If you say it's alright for your 16-year-old stepson to go out with his friends and be back by 10 p.m., but then your partner goes ahead and forbids him from being out later than 6 p.m., then the child is bound to become irritable about these conflicting rules.

Another thing to remember is that disagreements between parents regarding their parenting techniques and household rules leave a lot of room for manipulation by their children and stepchildren. It's not that difficult to put two arguing adults against each other so that the child may benefit in some way.

In order to live in a happy, blended household, there are a couple of things that you need to communicate about first. Remember, communication is always key!

Common Values

You and your partner should develop a list of household core values and display it in an area where it can be easily viewed and referred to. You can refer to the list of values that was included in an earlier chapter if you need some assistance. When drawing up your list, involve the whole family and make it a blended family bonding session. Gather the family in the living room or around the dining room table and explain that since you are going to be one family, it's important that you have a list of family values. Start off by mentioning some of the values that you think are important like honesty and kindness, then go around the table and ask everyone to mention at least two values that they think need to go on the list. Once everyone has listed their values and you have added it to the list, read out an extensive list of values, like the one included in the beginning of this book, and ask everyone to vote on each item as to whether they belong on the list of family values or not.

Once the list is compiled, make sure everyone at the table is happy with it, then go around and talk about examples where each of these values are challenged, trying to show the children exactly how to be steadfast in their values. Remember to keep the scenarios simple and easy to understand. For example, if you are challenging honesty, create a scenario where a friend asks one of the kids to lie to their parents about where they were and what they were doing. Explain that the family believes in honesty, that they should be honest about where they were and what they were doing, and always knowing where they are is important for their safety. Explain that you would only be disappointed if they were going against the values that you set out as a family. Being honest would also make them feel better than lying about where they were and what they were doing.

Household Rules

In the same way that you set out a list of family values, set out a list of household rules. Allow everyone to have a say, from your smallest stepchild to your teenager, and display the list in the most visible area of the house. You can decide as a family what goes on the list and make it clear that if rules are not adhered to, consequences will follow. In the list, you can include how much TV the kids are allowed to watch, how late the kids are allowed to stay out during week nights, and an allocation of household chores. In a blended household, when it comes to rules and consequences, the most important thing to remember is to treat all the kids alike. It's natural to want to make an extra effort with your stepchildren because they haven't known you for as long as your own children have, but when it comes to discipline, you need to show fairness and absolutely no favoritism. Getting your stepchild out of consequences because you want them to like you more is a sure way to be manipulated in the future.

While listing the rules, try to make a list of different grades of consequences as well. For example, an action like missing a chore can earn the punishment of an extra week of the same chore, instead of rotating into an easier chore. An action on the level of skipping school, however, can earn the punishment of a week of no TV. The severity of the action must match the punishment, and each level or grade of punishment needs to be consistent among all the children in the household.

Include yourself in the household rules to teach the family accountability as well, and let them know that you are all in this together. In addition, include yourself in the allocation of household chores, and if you are a particularly large family, you might want to choose teams to rotate the household chores. This way, you can be in a team with your stepchildren to build a deeper bond or connection.

It's extremely important to discuss and suggest household rules, disciplinary action, and more with your partner before calling the meeting to ensure that you both have an understanding as the figures of authority in the family. You don't want to be sitting at a table with your children and stepchildren, and it seems like you and your partner can't agree on a single thing.

Sometimes it might be better to let the child's biological parent take center stage when it comes to discipline, and as the stepparent, fall into the role of the copilot.

Connecting With Stepchildren

Stepchildren, like all children, are just that: children. They are still growing and developing, and the change in their family environment can be scary and overwhelming. A deep and meaningful relationship with stepchildren cannot be developed overnight. It takes time, and that does not mean just allowing time to pass by but really taking the time to actively engage with your stepchild and get to know them.

The tips that are outlined in the chapter on connecting with your child would work great for stepchildren as well, but where most stepparents go wrong is in their overcompensation for not being genetically related to the child. When you overcompensate, it comes across as overeager and sometimes, according to a few kids that I know, a little creepy. Give the child a little space as well—you are not the only one who has to adjust. The best way to connect with a stepchild is to spend time with them. Take them to the grocery store, invite them to cook with you, use car rides to get to know them, and try to show interest in their interests.

Routine is an important part of adjusting to a new home and living situation, especially if there's going to be movement from one house to another, like in the case of divorced parents. When the kids are moving from their other parent's house back to yours, include some sort of fun ritual or routine that helps in the transition. Take them out for lunch at their favorite restaurant before heading home, or take them all to watch a movie. It'll give them something to look forward to and remove the anxiety that usually comes with the adjustment.

The way children in a blended household interact with each other plays a huge role in the family setup. Children crave attention, and if your toddler feels neglected because you have to split your time between him and his new stepsister, he's bound to act out in ways that will negatively affect his relationship with his new sibling. The best way to prevent this from happening is to take some time to spend with each of your children individually. When it's time to play with your toddler, give him your undivided attention so that he still feels loved and cared for. Your original family still needs to understand how important they are to you. Spending all your time on building your relationships with your stepchildren can sort of diminish the relationships you already have with your own children.

Strengthen the Partnership

In a blended family household, the most important relationship to nurture is the one between you and your partner (Robinson, 2005). Take time and really communicate with your partner about your children and ask their advice where necessary. Remember, they know their own kids best, and you want to get to know their kids because they're part of your family now. Discuss any sort of family-related problems and brainstorm solutions together. Try to communicate honestly and openly while still respecting the other person's views and opinions that may differ from yours. Sometimes, even the way that you want to parent the children or handle a certain situation may differ. In these cases, it's important to come to some sort of compromise and consensus before involving the children. Children are also known to respect their parents and stepparents when they show a strong united front.

Divorce Doesn't Mean It's Over

If you have divorced your previous partner that you have children with, divorce doesn't mean that your relationship is over—it simply means that it's time for your relationship to change. Since there are children involved, it's safe to assume that your ex-partner is going to be in your life right until the end.

Keeping negative feelings about your ex-partner separate from the relationship you both share with your children is an absolutely vital part of keeping the peace within your household and your partners. It's important to try your best to develop a cordial understanding between yourself and your ex-partner. Furthermore, you should never badmouth or make negative comments about your ex-partner in front of your children or try to persuade them to view your ex in any kind of way. As hard as it might seem, sometimes you have to give your ex the benefit of the doubt.

Guard Against Ultimatums

Your children or your new partner may put you in a situation where you feel like you have to choose between them. You need to explain that whatever the problem, it is not your children against your partner but rather you all as a family working together to find a solution to a problem. You have to explain that they both hold a very special place in your life and that's not going to change any time soon.

Respect It, Even if You Don't Like It

When it comes to rules or even relationships between stepsiblings, not everyone is going to be on the same page and not everyone is going to like it. Even if two kids in the family haven't warmed up to each other yet, you can't force them to like each other. What you can insist on, however, is respect. Practicing respect toward one another is a good way to ease the transition into a newly blended household. Give it time. Soon enough, respect will grow into some sort of relationship—maybe not brotherhood, but even friendship is good enough. Remember, just a couple months ago these kids were strangers; give them time to warm up to each other.

Chapter 16:

Discipline Mistakes Parents Make

There's no such thing as a perfect parent, and most of the time, the really good parents who bring up healthy and happy individuals that live lives of success reached their parenting prime after a series of hits and misses. It's all trial and error—you have to try something in order to know if it works for you and your family. If not, then you can push it aside and move on to better things.

When it comes to discipline, there are many techniques that have been practiced in the past but have recently been studied and shown to have no positive impacts on the growth and development of the child. As parents, it's quite common to practice discipline techniques that your parents had practiced when you were a child. Sometimes, these techniques are in fact counterproductive to the disciplinary process and can lead to a strained parent-child relationship. Remember, even the best parents have to make mistakes in order to learn from them, so don't beat yourself up if parenting seems more difficult than usual at the moment. There are always going to be highs and lows, the important thing is to learn from the lows and really enjoy the highs.

Here are the 10 discipline mistakes that even the best parents make:

1. Setting Double Standards

When setting out rules for your household, it's important to understand that the rules are for everybody: you included. It's important that your children understand that nobody is above the rules, and you need to make sure that you are never caught breaking the rules. If your child witnesses you acting against the rules in any way, they could easily lose respect for you, they could begin to neglect the rules themselves, or they could even call you out on it. Trust me when

I say, respect is everything in a parent-child relationship, and you don't want to tamper with that. If your child calls you out on breaking the rules, it's going to be difficult to explain why you are allowed to do something that they are not, especially when you have written it down on the list of household rules. I'm not talking about having a glass of wine or watching TV after 10 p.m.—I'm talking about things like "No cell phones at the table during dinner" or "No talking over someone when they're telling a story."

It's important to lead by example when parenting because children do what they see. In fact, parents who say things like "because I'm a grown-up" or "I'm the adult" when children question why they are acting against the rules could have more strained relationships with their children. Their children regard them untrustworthy and begin to develop a sense of resentment from an early age. Try not to be all talk and no action. Show your child that you are in it just as much as they are; in fact, you are all in this together.

Parenting in this age can be particularly difficult if you have two children who are totally different in their personalities, interests, and abilities. Of course, as a good parent, you would want to tailor your parenting techniques to each of your children, but you have to remember that when it comes to discipline, fairness and equal treatment is key. If a consequence for not completing chores on time is one extra week of washing the dishes, you can't be compromising because the child finally got into the school orchestra and they need to rest their fingers to play the cello.

2. Disciplining for an Audience

One of the worst things that you can do for your child's confidence and self-esteem is to discipline them in front of others. If your child is behaving badly in public, try to diffuse the situation as smoothly as possible, and try your best not to lose your cool. I know it's easier said than done, but it's important in these situations that you remind yourself that the most important person around you right now is your child. The shop attendant that's packing the shelf close by and the man buying cereal further down the aisle both have very little impact on your life. What they think of your parenting or the way you handle the situation does not matter.

Shouting at your child in public, or even just around friends or family, might also lead them to focus less on what you are saying or trying to teach them, but more on who's around watching and what they think of them. Of course, if it's a life-or-death situation, shouting might be necessary, like if your child is about to jump off a swing while it's high in the air or if they're about to eat some sand from the sandbox.

Disciplining your children in front of others can cause them to develop defensive behaviors, and they may even grow to emotionally block you out, challenge your rules with aggressive behavior, or act out physically (Mombrite, 2018).

3. Giving Instruction Without Reason

Remember, your toddler's mind isn't developed enough to always understand what you are saying and why you are saying it, and your teenager is still learning about what the world is all about. Saying, "Stop throwing your clothes on the floor" or "Close the fridge after opening it" is easy enough to understand, but sometimes, you will need to explain why you want your children to carry out these actions. Explaining that they could potentially slip on their clothes and get hurt or that the food can spoil if the fridge is left open will help your child understand exactly why they need to practice this behavior. When children understand the reason behind the need for their actions, it helps develop their cognitive abilities; also, the habit is more likely to stick with them in the long run (Pfaff, 2017).

4. Using Negatives Instead of Positives

Believe it or not, understanding a negative is a relatively difficult thing for children, especially toddlers, simply because they might not have completely mastered the skill just yet. You have probably observed that telling your child not to do something just makes them want to do it more. This is because their attention is drawn to the main and exciting parts of your instructions and rarely the word "not." For example, when saying something like, "Please do not leave your wet raincoat on the couch," the parts that usually stick with the child are "raincoat" and "couch." You may go to the restroom and come back to the living room only to find that your toddler's wet coat has now soaked the couch. Using positives in instructions can be more effective as children are able to grasp the concept of the instructions much easier. For example, saying, "Please hang your wet raincoat on the hook outside to dry" might be a more effective way to prevent the couch from getting soaked.

In the same way, saying to your teenager, "Don't throw your stuff on the floor" might have the same effect. The negative instruction will seem to fly right over their head, and you will probably find yourself getting angry when you spot that jacket or backpack on the floor. Using a positive phrase like, "Hang your jacket on the hook and put your backpack in your room" might have a better effect.

5. Not Following Through

It's easy to feel sorry for your child and believe that they have learned their lesson by the second week of grounding and then let them off the hook for that final week, but you have to follow through with discipline! Not following through can leave you exposed and susceptible to manipulation in the future. In addition, if you don't stay true to your word, your child could lose a little bit of respect for you and fail to take you seriously in the future. You begin to lose your credibility.

Another thing to guard against is empty threats in order to frighten your child or get them to behave a little better. Rather than threatening, commit to a punishment if your child doesn't follow through with their good behavior. Remember, your job as a parent is to raise healthy, happy, and capable individuals who understand the importance of discipline. Your chosen punishment should be proportional to the child's behavior, and you need to make sure that the entire punishment is seen through until the end.

Be absolutely serious about the line between good and bad behavior (Living and Loving, 2019).

6. Letting Anger Get the Better of You

Trying to discipline a child while you are angry is like adding fuel to the fire. Nothing productive really comes from the situation. Take some time to calm yourself down before disciplining your child. Allow yourself to actually assess the situation to ensure that the punishment fits the behavior.

Often, when parents are angry while disciplining their children, they can be unfair in their punishment which can lead to a strained parent-child relationship in the long run.

7. Going on and On

Just as the punishment must fit the behavior, so must the lecture. Children often lose focus when parents tend to go into a lengthy lecture at any opportunity. Sometimes, discipline is more effective if you explain why what the child did was wrong and make it clear that they should not do it again (Pfaff, 2017).

This also applies to other situations where your child might come to you with a social problem or ask you for advice. Lecturing your child about the difference between right and wrong, every opportunity you get, can sometimes cause your child to become reluctant to openly communicate with you. The anticipation of that long lecture that they know is coming could lead your child to turn to a friend for advice on something important instead. This isn't necessarily a bad thing, but research has shown that it is as important for a parent to feel involved in their child's life as it is for a child to feel loved and appreciated. This kind of give and take will strengthen the parent-child relationship in the long run.

8. Disciplining When Discipline Is Not Necessary

To be clear, being annoyed at your children for being a little noisy or laughing too loud is not a cause for disciplinary action. This can cause children to become confused as to what they did wrong and make them irritated or agitated. In the long run, this also negatively affects the parent-child relationship and can lead to poor communication. Remember, children are just being themselves. They're exploring new skills and learning new things, so they're bound to get easily excited. When safety isn't an issue, learn to simply sit and watch without unnecessarily intervening. If your toddler wants to add orange juice instead of milk to their cereal, let them try out this new experience. Odds are, it'll make everyone happier than a screaming match followed by a tantrum. Observe and let them come to the conclusion themselves that milk might just be better. If your teenager is singing loudly in their room, and you have just had a long day at work and need some quiet time, close their room door and yours, and center yourself rather than shouting and demanding that they stop.

9. Being Fixed in Your Parenting Ways

As your child grows, they're bound to have more experiences that you would have at their age. This idea that they have been exposed to more than might change their opinions and views of the world. Older children will challenge your beliefs and opinions, but the most important thing to trust in is the values that you have instilled in them.

Being able to adapt your parenting ways to the new age of growing children is a must in the current times. You have to remember that ideas about sex and other formerly taboo social topics are not spoken about openly and might be a part of your child's life once they reach a certain age. Disciplining your child for normal developmental changes such as newfound sexual urges and making such topics prohibited in your household will negatively affect your child's development. I'm not saying that you should openly talk about drugs and sex at the dinner table; what I'm saying is that your child may engage in such activity with or without your knowledge. As a parent, you need to be able to be open and honest, and provide your child with the right advice in order to ensure that they are always safe and can still come to you to talk about anything at all. No subject should be off-limits between a parent and child, even if it causes you discomfort.

10. Fighting Every Battle That Comes Your Way

Picking your battles is important to ensure that you don't exhaust yourself by excessive parenting. By not choosing your battles and picking on everything that comes your way, you are bound to spend more time pointing out our poor behavior than enjoying your child's company or building your relationship. Constant nagging becomes annoying and can seriously negatively affect a parent-child relationship. Think about it: Would you want to spend time with someone who's constantly picking on everything that you do wrong?

Weigh the pros and cons before deciding to pick a fight. Remember, you want to create a positive environment for your children. Constantly criticizing them is bound to cause them to hide things from you and feel constant disappointment, which is bad for their self-esteem and could make them feel self-conscious. Some battles are just not worth it.

Conclusion

As parents, we all want the best for our children. We strive to raise talented children who will go on to enjoy happy lives and be morally upright. However, we occasionally find ourselves second-guessing our parenting decisions, crossing our fingers, and praying we're doing everything properly. Our goals, dreams, and worries about parenting will never fade away, but it turns out that we no longer have to wing it and rely solely on hope. We now have a scientific plan for raising well-balanced, caring, and emotionally intelligent children thanks to emotion training, and this book guides you about just that. This book teaches you and your children how to utilize emotion coaching to work through their emotions: sadness, anger, and confusion.

The thing is, being a parent means that you spend most of the time teaching, reminding, scolding, yelling, and reprimanding, all for good reason of course. You want your child to be the best version of themselves possible, and to do that, you need to make sure that they're learning and practicing all the important stuff, like good behavior and the difference between right and wrong. If you find yourself engaging in too much nagging or shouting, take a break and try to make a positive connection with your child, even if it seems difficult to wrap your head around it in the moments building up to it. Remember, you are doing the best you can, so don't beat yourself up for having those days where you don't have the patience for the crying and the tantrums. One day at a time.

There are ways to connect with your child while still maintaining boundaries and your position of authority. Every moment is an opportunity to connect with your child, even those moments of anger and frustration or when your child is throwing the mother of all tantrums. Take a deep breath, remember how much you love that little monster, and then proceed appropriately but with caution. Remember to engage in the conversation as well. Prompt your child by asking questions and letting them know that you really are interested and want to know about their opinions and their newfound beliefs.

Healthy human emotions have a tendency to flow through us, overwhelm us, and then go away. When we ward them off or suppress them, emotions become stuck inside us instead of finding healthy expressions. Children, on the other hand, are afraid of their intense emotions dominating them, so they strive to avoid them until they feel comfortable enough to face them. Outbursts are nature's way of helping young children express their emotions because feelings are stored in the body. When we make them feel comfortable enough to experience and show their feelings, we not only soothe our children's thought processes and bodies, we also teach them to trust their own emotional expression so that they can manage their own feelings as they grow older without tantrums or repression.

This book teaches you all about connecting with your child through different techniques. Sharing work and life stories with your child is a great way of allowing them to be involved in all aspects of your life. Believe it or not, children who know the name of their parents' bosses and work colleagues are known to feel closer to their parents and more involved in their lives. It's important to remember that we are all human, and sometimes, after a long tiring day at school, your teenager may not really want to sit down and get into details about their day. That's alright: Give them the space that they need, and let them know that whenever they're ready to talk, they know where to find you. Snuggling with your child is another great way to build a strong bond and connection. The power of physical contact and touch is covered in a later chapter, but basically holding your child will comfort them and has shown to increase happiness and self-worth. It's difficult to understand the feelings that appear unreasonable or absurd when our children do or say things that are completely undesirable. However, try to picture yourself in your kid's shoes. Ask questions, seek knowledge, and let them know you're on their side, that you support them, and that you'll be there to hold their hand during the difficult times.

No matter how important emotion training is, being a little strict and setting boundaries are important, too. It's time to put things right after you've listened empathically, recognized feelings, and established limitations on any harmful behavior. Someone needs to take charge of the problem-solving process. That person isn't you, by the way. This is another ability you should assist them in developing. You won't always be around to direct their actions. Motivate them to come up with new ideas and lead them to a strategy that is productive and puts other people's feelings into account, all while being true to your principles. This is how emotionally intelligent children develop into resourceful and responsible young adults.

Parenting is a demanding and never-ending job. You can raise children who are clever, self-assured, and better able to handle the complexities of life with ease and confidence by taking just the actions mentioned in the book.

All youngsters experience strong emotions on a regular basis. They frequently feel weak and pushed around, as well as angry, unhappy, fearful, or jealous. Emotionally healthy children process their feelings through play, which is how all young children learn. By assisting your child in "playing out" his major inner conflicts, he will be able to resolve them and progress to the next age-appropriate growth challenge

Even most adults find it difficult to express their deepest emotional struggles into words, and your child is no exception. He can, however, play them out metaphorically and resolve them without having to discuss them. They frequently feel weak and pushed around, as well as angry, unhappy, fearful, or jealous.

There is always room for improvement, no matter how emotionally intelligent your child appears to be. There will very certainly be highs and lows during childhood and youth. As they get older, they'll certainly confront challenges that will test their abilities. As a result, make it a priority to incorporate skill development into your daily routine. Talk about emotions with your child every day when he or she is young. Discuss the feelings that characters in novels or movies might be experiencing. Discuss alternative solutions to challenges or tactics that characters could employ to treat each other with respect.

Make the most of your child's mistakes to help him or her improve. Find a chance to interact about how they can do better for the future when they lash out when they're angry or they upset someone's feelings. Your child can build the emotional intelligence and inner resilience they'll need to lead a good life if they have your continuing support and direction. Giving your children the space to comprehend and convey their own feelings is the key to raising children who appreciate and sympathize with others' feelings. If you provide a listening ear to hear about their frustrations or fears, your children will learn how to deal with emotional distress by expressing it to you, a therapist, or even a journal gifted by you. Perhaps more importantly, they'll realize that the best approach to deal with other people's bad feelings is to recognize them and work through them.

This book works as a road map to show you how to teach your kids to breathe through their emotions, to experience them, to accept them without acting on them, and to problem solve and respond if needed after they are no longer overwhelmed by powerful emotions. Children who can detect their own feelings are more likely to be willing to articulate what they require in order to maintain their composure. This is fantastic news for parents since it not only encourages healthy growth, but it also means less tantrums, power battles, and whining. When children believe their emotions are understood and appreciated, the sentiments usually lose their power and dissolve. This creates an opportunity to solve an issue. This is something that children can do on their own at times. They may require your assistance in brainstorming at times. However, unless they specifically ask for it, resist the impulse to rush in and solve the problem for them; doing so sends the message that you don't trust his capacity to do it on his own.

Thank you once again for reading this book. If you enjoyed it, please feel free to leave a review on Amazon or Audible.

References

AdventHealth. (2019). Developing Children's Motor Skills Through Cooking. Myhealthkc.com. https://myhealthkc.com/blog/developing-childrens-motor-skills-through-cooking

American Academy of Pediatrics. (2019). What's the Best Way to Discipline My Child? HealthyChildren.org. https://www.healthychildren.org/English/family-life/family-dynamics/communication-discipline/Pages/Disciplining-Your-Child.aspx

Arslan, M. (2013). EMOTIONAL INTELLIGENCE AND IMPORTANCE FOR CHILDREN. Journal of International Management, Educational and Economics Perspectives, 1(2)(P36). https://www.academia.edu/35019294/EMOTIONAL_INTELLIGENCE_AND_IMPORTANCE_FOR_CHILDREN

Bar-On, Reuven. (2006). The Bar-On Model of Emotional-Social Intelligence. Psicothema. 18 Suppl. 13-25.

Bitbrain. (2019, March 29). What are emotions and feelings, and how to measure them? Bitbrain. https://www.bitbrain.com/blog/difference-feelings-emotions

Blended Learning. (2011). Cognitive Scaffolding Strategies - Blended Learning. Sites.google.com. https://sites.google.com/site/arifinblended/home/page_9/page_9-2

Boyatzis, R. E., & Sala, F. (2004). The Emotional Competence Inventory (ECI). In G. Geher (Ed.), Measuring emotional intelligence: Common ground and controversy (pp. 147–180). Nova Science Publishers.

Brackett, M. (2009). Emotional Intelligence. Noba. https://nobaproject.com/modules/emotional-intelligence

Butler, C. (2020, November 8). Is Your Child Manipulative? 5 Helpful Strategies. Quick and Dirty Tips. https://www.quickanddirtytips.com/parenting/behavior/manipulative-child

Cherry, K. (2013, October 11). IQ vs. EQ: Which One Is More Important? Verywell Mind; Verywellmind. https://www.verywellmind.com/iq-or-eq-which-one-is-more-important-2795287

Cherry, K. (2019, July 17). Uninvolved Parenting and Its Effects on Children. Verywell Mind. https://www.verywellmind.com/what-is-uninvolved-parenting-2794958#:~:text=Uninvolved%20parenting%2C%20sometimes%20referred%20to

Cherry, K. (2020, June 3). Overview of Emotional Intelligence. Verywell Mind; Verywellmind. https://www.verywellmind.com/what-is-emotional-intelligence-2795423

Encyclopedia Britannica. (2019). Wernicke area | anatomy. In Encyclopædia Britannica. https://www.britannica.com/science/Wernicke-area

First Things First. (2018). Brain Development - First Things First. First Things First. https://www.firstthingsfirst.org/early-childhood-matters/brain-development/

Fisher, D., & Frey, N. (2010). Scaffolds for Learning: The Key to Guided Instruction. Ascd.org. http://www.ascd.org/publications/books/111017/chapters/Scaffolds-for-Learning@-The-Key-to-Guided-Instruction.aspx

Freedman, J. (2017, May 15). What's the Difference Between Emotion, Feeling, Mood? Six Seconds. https://www.6seconds.org/2017/05/15/emotion-feeling-mood/#:~:text=Emotions%20are%20chemicals%20released%20in

Gottman, J. M., Declaire, J., & Goleman, D. (2015). Raising an emotionally intelligent child. New York, N.Y. Simon & Schuster Paperbacks.

Hallet, K. (2020, December 20). There Are 7 Different Types Of Hugs: Here's The Meaning Behind Each One (A. Moore, Ed.). Mindbodygreen. https://www.mindbodygreen.com/articles/types-of-hugs

Harrington, R. G. (2004). NASP Center - Parents' Guide to Temper Tantrums. Www.naspcenter.org. http://www.naspcenter.org/parents/tantrums_ho.html

Harvard University. (2019). InBrief: The Science of Early Childhood Development. Center on the Developing Child at Harvard University. https://developingchild.harvard.edu/resources/inbrief-science-of-ecd/

Headway. (2018). Lobes of the brain and their functions. Headway Ireland. https://headway.ie/about-the-brain/lobes-of-the-brain/

Herculano-Houzel, S. (2009). The human brain in numbers: a linearly scaled-up primate brain. Frontiers in Human Neuroscience, 3. https://doi.org/10.3389/neuro.09.031.2009

Higuera, V. (2019, September 12). Helicopter Parenting: What It Is and Pros and Cons. Healthline. https://www.healthline.com/health/parenting/helicopter-parenting#what-it-looks-like

Hughes, S., Lyddy, F., & Lambe, S. (2013). Misconceptions about Psychological Science: A Review. Psychology Learning & Teaching, 12(1), 20–31. https://doi.org/10.2304/plat.2013.12.1.20

JAMES, W. (1884). II.—WHAT IS AN EMOTION ? Mind, os-IX(34), 188–205. https://doi.org/10.1093/mind/os-ix.34.188

Jarvis, A., & Roffe, R. (2020). Parenting with Purpose (p.). Amazon Publishing.

John Hopkins Medicine. (2019). Anatomy of the Brain. Johns Hopkins Medicine. https://www.hopkinsmedicine.org/health/conditions-and-diseases/anatomy-of-the-brain

Johnson, J. (2020, May 22). Occipital lobe: Definition, function, and linked conditions. Www.medicalnewstoday.com. https://www.medicalnewstoday.com/articles/occipital-lobe#definition

Kanoy, K. (2013). The everything parent's guide to emotional intelligence in children : how to raise children who are caring, resilient, and emotionally strong. Adams Media.

King James Bible. (2013). Christian Art Gifts. (Original work published 1611).

Lee, K. (2021, April). Strategies for Setting Healthy Boundaries for Kids. Verywell Family. https://www.verywellfamily.com/whos-the-boss-how-to-set-healthy-boundaries-for-kids-3956403

Lenroot, R. K., & Giedd, J. N. (2006). Brain development in children and adolescents: Insights from anatomical magnetic resonance imaging. Neuroscience & Biobehavioral Reviews, 30(6), 718–729. https://doi.org/10.1016/j.neubiorev.2006.06.001

Lindebaum, D., & Jordan, P. J. (2012). Positive emotions, negative emotions, or utility of discrete emotions? Journal of Organizational Behavior, 33(7), 1027–1030. https://doi.org/10.1002/job.1819

Livesey, P. (2017). Goldman-Boyatzis Model of Emotional Intelligence for Dealing with Problems in Project Management. Construction Economics and Building. 17. 20. 10.5130/AJCEB.v17i1.5101.

Living And Loving Staff. (2019, June 14). 7 discipline mistakes parents make and how to fix them. All4Women. https://www.all4women.co.za/2141038/parenting/pre-schooler-4-6/7-discipline-mistakes-parents-make-fix

McAdams, T. A., Rijsdijk, F. V., Narusyte, J., Ganiban, J. M., Reiss, D., Spotts, E., Neiderhiser, J. M., Lichtenstein, P., & Eley, T. C. (2016). Associations between the parent-child relationship and adolescent self-worth: a genetically informed study of twin parents and their adolescent children. Journal of Child Psychology and Psychiatry, 58(1), 46–54. https://doi.org/10.1111/jcpp.12600

McEwen B. S. (2011). Effects of stress on the developing brain. Cerebrum : the Dana forum on brain science, 2011, 14.

McLaughlin, K. A., Sheridan, M. A., & Lambert, H. K. (2014). Childhood adversity and neural development: deprivation and threat as distinct dimensions of early experience. Neuroscience and biobehavioral reviews, 47, 578–591. https://doi.org/10.1016/j.neubiorev.2014.10.012

Mombrite. (2018, June 4). 12 Biggest Mistakes Parents Make when Disciplining Children | Mombrite. Www.mombrite.com. https://www.mombrite.com/disciplining-children/

Morin, A. (2019a). 6 Parenting Strategies for Raising Emotionally Intelligent Kids. Verywell Family.

https://www.verywellfamily.com/tips-for-raising-an-emotionally-intelligent-child-4157946

Morin, A. (2019b, July 16). 4 types of parenting styles and their effects on kids. Verywell Family; Verywellfamily. https://www.verywellfamily.com/types-of-parenting-styles-1095045

Morin, A. (2020, November 21). How Free-Range Parenting Can Benefit Your Child. Verywell Family. https://www.verywellfamily.com/what-is-free-range-parenting-1095057

Morin, A. (2021, May 9). 5 Positive Discipline Techniques to Try. VeryWellFamily. https://www.verywellfamily.com/examples-of-positive-discipline-1095049

National Institute of Neurological Disorders and Stroke. (2020). Brain Basics: Know Your Brain | National Institute of Neurological Disorders and Stroke. Nih.gov. https://www.ninds.nih.gov/Disorders/Patient-Caregiver-Education/Know-Your-Brain#:~:text=The%20brain%20is%20the%20most

National Research Council (US) and Institute of Medicine (US) Committee on Integrating the Science of Early Childhood Development, Shonkoff, J. P., & Phillips, D. A. (Eds.). (2000). From Neurons to Neighborhoods: The Science of Early Childhood Development. National Academies Press (US).

Paavola, L. (2017). The importance of emotional intelligence in early childhood.

Perry, C. (2019, December 6). Authoritarian Parenting: The Pros and Cons, According to a Child Psychologist. Parents; Parents. https://www.parents.com/parenting/better-parenting/style/authoritarian-parenting-the-pros-and-cons-according-to-a-child-psychologist/

Pfaff, L. G. (2017). 10 Biggest Discipline Mistakes You're Probably Making. Parents. https://www.parents.com/parenting/better-parenting/advice/biggest-discipline-mistakes-youre-probably-making/

Pozatek, K. (2015, June 18). mindbodygreen. Mindbodygreen. https://www.mindbodygreen.com/0-17051/why-its-important-to-set-healthy-boundaries-with-your-kids.html

Reigeluth, C. (1999). Instructional-design theories and models, Vol. II: A new paradigm of instructional theory (92).

Robinson, H. (2005, October 3). A Blended Family United: Tips for Overcoming Issues Together. Parents; Parents. https://www.parents.com/parenting/divorce/blended-families/navigating-the-challenges-of-blended-families/

Sarikas, C. (2018). Vygotsky Scaffolding: What It Is and How to Use It. Prepscholar.com. https://blog.prepscholar.com/vygotsky-scaffolding-zone-of-proximal-development

Sarkadi, A., Kristiansson, R., Oberklaid, F., & Bremberg, S. (2008). Fathers' involvement and children's developmental outcomes: a systematic review of longitudinal studies. Acta paediatrica (Oslo, Norway : 1992), 97(2), 153–158. https://doi.org/10.1111/j.1651-2227.2007.00572.x

Sege, R. D., & Siegel, B. S. (2018). Effective Discipline to Raise Healthy Children. Pediatrics, 142(6), e20183112. https://doi.org/10.1542/peds.2018-3112

Seladi-Schulman, J. (2020, April 20). What to Know About Your Brain's Frontal Lobe. Healthline. https://www.healthline.com/health/frontal-lobe

Shmerling, R. H. (2017, July 28). Right brain/left brain, right? - Harvard Health Blog. Harvard Health Blog. https://www.health.harvard.edu/blog/right-brainleft-brain-right-2017082512222

SixSeconds. (2019). Parenting with Emotional Intelligence • Six
Seconds EQ. Six Seconds.
https://www.6seconds.org/parenting/

Stiles, J., & Jernigan, T. L. (2010). The Basics of Brain Development.
Neuropsychology Review, 20(4), 327–348.
https://doi.org/10.1007/s11065-010-9148-4

The Brain From Top to Bottom. (2019). BROCA'S AREA ,
WERNICKE'S AREA, AND OTHER LANGUAGE-
PROCESSING AREAS IN THE BRAIN. Mcgill.ca.
https://thebrain.mcgill.ca/flash/d/d_10/d_10_cr/d_10_cr_la
n/d_10_cr_lan.html

The Editors of Encyclopedia Britannica. (2016). Midbrain | anatomy.
In Encyclopædia Britannica.
https://www.britannica.com/science/midbrain

The Urban Child Institute. (2009). Baby's Brain Begins Now:
Conception to Age 3. Urbanchildinstitute.org.
http://www.urbanchildinstitute.org/why-0-3/baby-and-brain

TOMINEY, S. L., O'BRYON, E. C., RIVERS, S. E., & SHAPSES, S.
(2017). Teaching Emotional Intelligence in Early Childhood |
NAEYC. Naeyc.org.
https://www.naeyc.org/resources/pubs/yc/mar2017/teaching
-emotional-intelligence

Underwood, P. L. (2020, May 8). A Field Guide to Taming Tantrums
in Toddlers. The New York Times.
https://www.nytimes.com/article/temper-tantrum.html

Vandergriendt, C. (2018). What Is a Neuron? Function, Parts,
Structure, Types, and More. Healthline.
https://www.healthline.com/health/neurons

Wright, L. W. (2019). 8 Quick Ways to Connect Meaningfully With
Your Child. Www.understood.org.
https://www.understood.org/en/learning-thinking-

differences/understanding-childs-challenges/simple-changes-at-home/8-quick-ways-time-strapped-parents-can-connect-meaningfully-with-their-kids

Wessel, L. (2019). The First Years of Life. Brainfacts.org. https://www.brainfacts.org/thinking-sensing-and-behaving/brain-development/2019/the-first-years-of-life-092419

West, A., Swanson, J., & Lipscomb, L. (2017). Ch. 11 Scaffolding. Granite.pressbooks.pub. https://granite.pressbooks.pub/teachingdiverselearners/chapter/scaffolding-2/

Yale Center. (2020). RULER. Yale Center for Emotional Intelligence. https://www.ycei.org/ruler

Zhang, F., Parmley, M., Wan, X., & Cavanagh, S. (2014). Cultural differences in recognition of subdued facial expressions of emotions. Motivation and Emotion, 39(2), 309–319. https://doi.org/10.1007/s11031-014-9454-x

www.ingramcontent.com/pod-product-compliance
Lightning Source LLC
Chambersburg PA
CBHW080419030426
42335CB00020B/2511